Irish Fairy Tales

IRISH FAIRY TALES

Edited by LESLIE CONRON

Madison Park Press

Developed by Arena Books Associates, LLC.

This edition published by Madison Park Press
by arrangement with Arena Books Associates, LLC.

Photographs from The Irish Image Collection.

Copyright © 2006 Madison Park Press

ISBN:1-58288-213-4

Sources:
Yeats's collection (*Fairy and Folk Tales of the Irish Peasantry*) includes tales from many sources, including many that we have included in this collection. Tales in this book credited to Carleton, Hyde, Allingham, Kennedy, and Todhunter have been taken from Yeats's 1888 collection. The tales we have included from Croker, Lover, Curtin, and Wilde have been taken from the appropriate sources listed below.

Thomas Crofton Croker. *Fairy Legends and Traditions of the South of Ireland,* 1825.
Jeremiah Curtin. *Myths and Folk-Lore of Ireland*, 1890.
Samuel Lover. *Legends and Stories of Ireland,*1837.
Lady Wilde. *Ancient Legends of Ireland,*1887.

W. B. Yeats. *Fairy and Folk Tales of the Irish Peasantry,*1888. (This is Yeats's previously mentioned collection of tales from a variety of sources.)

W. B. Yeats. *The Celtic Twilight: Myth, Fantasy, and Folklore,* 1893. (Yeats's own stories along with his poetic interpretations of the world of Faery. The three Yeats selections we have included have been taken from this book.)

Contents

Introduction

Tales of enchantment and magic have fascinated us all—young and old alike—for hundreds of years. Tales that transport us to a world where anything can happen ignite our imaginations. From earliest times, the Irish have been weaving spells by telling fabulous tales. Itinerant travelers were welcomed into homes for a warm fire and a few nights lodging in exchange for evenings of diversion, telling stories by the fire. Storytellers would gather of an evening to offer their stories, and if more than one version of a story was told, the versions would be voted on and the tellers would have to abide by the verdict. And thus the stories have been handed down with accuracy.

In the nineteenth century several Irish story-lovers transcribed the tales as they were told by the tellers. Some of the best-known collections are those of Samuel Lover and

Thomas Crofton Croker (1825), William Carleton (1830), Patrick Kennedy (1866), William Butler Yeats (1888,1892), Douglas Hyde (1890), Jeremiah Curtin (1890). We have included selections from each of them, in addition to works of Letitia Maclintock, Lady Wilde, and William Allingham.

We are shown the range of Irish storytelling, from the mischievous pranksters and practical jokers to the capricious and sometimes mean-spirited puchas (pookas), from the industrious, shoe-making leprechauns with their hidden crocks of gold, to the changelings, keening banshees, and the merrows (mermaids, who fishermen fear seeing because they bring stormy weather). Not always small, the fairies can take on a size and shape that suits their whim. And not always good, some fairies steal new brides or new babies to bring back with them to their world.

And who are the fairies? Fallen angels, gods of the earth, or gods of pagan Ireland are some suggestions offered to us. WIlliam Butler Yeats, in his *Fairy and Folk Tales of Ireland*, tells us that they are "beings so quickly offended that you must not speak much about them at all, and never call them anything but the 'gentry,' or else *daoine maithe*, which in English means 'good people,' yet so easily pleased they will do their best to keep misfortune away from you, if you leave a little milk for them on the windowsill over night. "

In these tales, you will find characters you know and

some you don't, tales that are familiar (the Irish version of the Cinderella tale, for example), and some that are not. And you will find magic swords, battles with giants, cloaks of invisibility, appearing- and disappearing-lands of eternal youth beneath the water, fairy "spells" that last anywhere from a year and a day to twenty, thirty, or one hundred years and a day, animals that have strange powers, and humans that take the form of animals.

Read aloud, as these tales were meant to be, you can feel the music of the language, the thought, and the spirit. Let the sound of the language transport you, tell you what a word means. Hear it with your mind's ear. Savor the lilting melodies and colorful expressions gathered from this wonderful oral tradition. And when you read the stories aloud you will find the occasional unfamiliar word understandable, as if you'd always known that "ainsel" was one's "own self," or "praties" were "potatoes," or that a "th" and a "d" can be transposed as in "murtherer or "wid."

And when the wind swirls the leaves outside your window, or bends the flowers at your door, imagine that the fairies are bringing a little magic into your world.

NOTE: Because the sources for these tales are many, there are variations in the spelling and use of words.

The Priest's Supper
Thomas Crofton Croker

It is said by those who ought to understand such things, that the good people, or the fairies, are some of the angels who were turned out of heaven, and who landed on their feet in this world, while the rest of their companions, who had more sin to sink them, went down farther to a worse place. Be this as it may, there was a merry troop of the fairies, dancing and playing all manner of wild pranks on a bright moonlight evening towards the end of September. The scene of their merriment was not far distant from Inchegeela, in the west of the county Cork—a poor village, although it had a barrack for soldiers; but great mountains and barren rocks, like those round about it, are enough to strike poverty into any place. However as the fairies can have everything they want for wishing, poverty does not trouble them much, and all their care is to seek out unfrequented nooks and places where it is not likely any one will come to spoil their sport.

On a nice green sod by the river's side were the little fellows dancing in a ring as gaily as may be, with their red caps wagging about at every bound in the moonshine, and so light were these bounds that the lobes of dew, although they trembled under their feet, were not disturbed by their capering. Thus did they carry on their gambols, spinning round and round, and twirling and bobbing and diving, and going through all manner of figures, until one of them chirped out,

"Cease, cease, with your drumming,
Here's an end to our mumming;
By my smell
I can tell
A priest this way is coming!"

And away every one of the fairies scampered off as hard as they could, concealing themselves under the green leaves of the lusmore, where, if their little red caps should happen to peep out, they would only look like its crimson bells; and more hid themselves in the hollow of stones, or at the shady side of brambles, and others under the bank of the river, and in holes and crannies of one kind or another.

The fairy speaker was not mistaken; for along the road,

which was within view of the river, came Father Horrigan on his pony, thinking to himself that as it was so late he would make an end of his journey at the first cabin he came to. According to his determination, he stopped at the dwelling of Dermod Leary, lifted the latch, and entered with "My blessing on all here."

I need not say that Father Horrigan was a welcome guest wherever he went, for no man was more pious or better beloved in the country. Now it was a great trouble to Dermod that he had nothing to offer his reverence for supper as a relish to the potatoes, which "the old woman"—for so Dermod called his wife, though she was not much past twenty—had down boiling in a pot over the fire. He thought of the net which he had set in the river, but as it had been there only a short time, the chances were against his finding a fish in it. "No matter," thought Dermod, "there can be no harm in stepping down to try; and maybe, as I want the fish for the priest's supper, that one will be there before me."

Down to the river-side went Dermod, and he found in the net as fine a salmon as ever jumped in the bright waters of "the spreading Lee"; but as he was going to take it out, the net was pulled from him—he could not tell how or by whom—and away got the salmon, and went swimming along with the current as gaily as if nothing had happened.

Dermod looked sorrowfully at the wake which the fish had left upon the water, shining like a line of silver in the moonlight, and then, with an angry motion of his right hand and a stamp of his foot, gave vent to his feelings by muttering: "May bitter bad luck attend you night and day for a blackguard schemer of a salmon, wherever you go! You ought to be ashamed of yourself, if there's any shame in you, to give me the slip after this fashion! And I'm clear in my own mind you'll come to no good, for some kind of evil thing or other helped you. Did I not feel it pull the net against me as strong as the devil himself?"

"That's not true for you," said one of the little fairies who had scampered off at the approach of the priest, coming up to Dermod Leary, with a whole throng of companions at his heels; "there was only a dozen and a half of us pulling against you."

Dermod gazed on the tiny speaker with wonder, who continued, "Make yourself noways uneasy about the priest's supper; for if you will go back and ask him one question from us, there will be as fine a supper as ever was put on a table, spread out before him in less than no time."

"I'll have nothing at all to do with you," replied Dermod in a tone of determination, and after a pause he added: "I'm much obliged to you for your offer, sir, but I know better than to sell myself to you, or the likes of you, for a supper; and more than that, I know Father Horrigan has more regard for my soul than to wish me to pledge it for ever, out of regard to anything you could put before him— so there's an end of the matter."

The little speaker, with a pertinacity not to be repulsed

by Dermod's manner, continued: "Will you ask the priest one civil question for us?"

Dermod considered for some time, and he was right in doing so, but he thought that no one could come to harm out of asking a civil question. "I see no objection to do that same, gentlemen," said Dermod: "but I will have nothing in life to do with your supper—mind that."

"Then," said the little speaking fairy, whilst the rest came crowding after him from all parts, "go and ask Father Horrigan to tell us whether our souls will be saved at the last day, like the souls of good Christians; and if you wish us well, bring back word what he says without delay."

Away went Dermod to his cabin, where he found the potatoes thrown out on the table, and his good woman handing the biggest of them all—a beautiful, laughing, red apple, smoking like a hard-ridden horse on a frosty night—over to Father Horrigan.

"Please your reverence," said Dermod, after some hesitation, "may I make bold to ask your honour one question?"

"What may that be?" said Father Horrigan.

"Why, then, begging your reverence's pardon for my freedom, it is, If the souls of the good people are to be saved at the last day?"

"Who bid you ask me that question, Leary?" said the priest, fixing his eyes upon him very sternly, which Dermod could not stand before at all.

"I'll tell no lies about the matter, and nothing in life but the truth," said Dermod. "It was the good people themselves who sent me to ask the question, and there they are in thousands down on the bank of the river, waiting for me to go back with the answer."

"Go back by all means," said the priest, "and tell them, if they want to know, to come here to me themselves, and I'll answer that or any other question they are pleased to ask, with the greatest pleasure in life."

Dermod accordingly returned to the fairies, who came swarming round about him to hear what the priest had said in reply, and Dermod spoke out among them like a bold man as he was; but when they heard that they must go to the priest, away they fled, some here and more there, and some this way and more that, whisking by poor Dermod so fast, and in such numbers, that he was quite bewildered.

When he came to himself, which was not for a long time, back he went to his cabin and ate his dry potatoes along with Father Horrigan, who made quite light of the thing; but Dermod could not help thinking it a mighty hard case that his reverence, whose words had the power to banish the fairies at such a rate, should have no sort of relish to his supper, and that the fine salmon he had in the net should have been got away from him in such a manner.

A Teller of Tales
William Butler Yeats

Many of the tales in this
book* were told me by one Paddy Flynn, a little bright-eyed
old man, who lived in a leaky and one-roomed cabin in the village of Ballisodare, which is, he was wont to say, 'the most
gentle' —whereby he meant faery—'place in the whole of
County Sligo.' Others hold it, however, but second to Drumcliff
and Drumahair. The first time I saw him he was cooking
mushrooms for himself; the next time he was asleep under a
hedge, smiling in his sleep. He was indeed always cheerful,
though I thought I could see in his eyes (swift as the eyes of a
rabbit, when they peered out of their wrinkled holes) a melancholy which was well-nigh a porion of their joy; the visionary
melancholy of purely instinctive natures and of all animals.

And yet there was much in his life to depress him, for in the triple solitude of age, eccentricity, and deafness, he went about much pestered by children. It was for this very reason perhaps that he ever recommended mirth and hopefulness. He was fond, for instance, of telling how Columcille cheered up his mother. 'How are you today, mother?' said the saint. 'Worse,' replied the mother. 'May you be worse tomorrow,' said the saint. The next day Columcille came again, and exactly the same conversation took place, but the third day the mother said, 'Better, thank God.' And the saint replied, 'May you be better tomorrow.' He was fond too of telling how the Judge smiles at the last day alike when he rewards the good and condemns the lost to unceasing flames. He had many strange sights to keep him cheerful or to make him sad. I asked him had he ever seen the faeries, and got the reply, 'Am I not annoyed with them?' I asked too if he had ever seen the banshee, 'I have seen it,' he said, 'down there by the water, batting the river with its hands.'

I have copied this account from Paddy Flynn, with a few verbal alterations, from a note-book which I almost filled with his tales and sayings, shortly after seeing him. I look now at the note-book gratefully, for the blank pages at the end will never be filled up. Paddy Flynn is dead; a friend of mine gave him a large bottle of whiskey, and though a sober man at most times, the sight of so much liquor filled him with great enthusiasm, and he lived upon it some days and then died. His body, worn out with old age and hard times, could not bear the drink as in his young days. He was a great teller of tales, and unlike our common romancers, knew how to employ heaven, hell, and purgatory, faeryland and earth, to people his stories. He did not live in a shrunken world, but knew of no less ample circumstance than did Homer himself. Perhaps the Gaelic people shall by his like bring back again the ancient simplicity and amplitude of imagination. What is literature but the expression of moods by the vehicle of symbol and incident? And are there not moods which need heaven, hell, purgatory, and faeryland for their expression, no less than this dilapidated earth? Nay, are there not moods which shall find no expression unless there be men who dare to mix heaven, hell, purgatory, and faeryland together, or even to set the heads of beasts to the bodies of men, or to thrust the souls of men into the heart of rocks? Let us go forth, the teller of tales, and seize whatever prey the heart long for, and have no fear. Everything exists, everything is true, and the earth is only a little dust under our feet.

Kidnappers

William Butler Yeats

A little north of the town of Sligo, on the southern side of Ben Bulben, some hundreds of feet above the plain, is a small white square in the limestone. No mortal has ever touched it with his hand; no sheep or goat has ever browsed grass beside it. There is no more inaccessible place upon the earth, and few more encircled by awe to the deep considering. It is the door of faery-land. In the middle of night it swings open, and the unearthly troop rushes out. All night the gay rabble sweep to and fro across the land, invisible to all, unless perhaps where, in some more than commonly 'gentle' place— Drumcliff or Drum-a-hair—the night-capped heads of faery-doctors may be thrust from their doors to see what mischief the 'gentry' are doing. To their trained eyes and ears the fields are covered by red-hatted riders, and the air is full of shrill voices—a sound like whistling, as an ancient Scottish seer has recorded, and wholly different from the talk of the angels, who 'speak much in the throat, like the Irish, as Lilly, the astrologer, has wisely said. If there be a new-born baby or new-wed bride in the neighbourhood, the night-capped 'doctors' will peer with more than common care, for the unearthly troop do not always return empty-handed. . Sometimes a new-wed bride or a new-born baby goes with them into their mountains; the door swings to behind, and the new-born or the new-wed moves henceforth in the bloodless land of Faery; happy enough, but doomed to melt out at the last judgment like bright vapour, for the soul cannot live without sorrow. Through this door of white stone, and the other doors of that land where *geabheadth tu an sonas aer pighin* ('you can buy joy for a penny'), have gone kings, queens, and princes, but so greatly has the power of Faery dwindled, that there are none but peasants in these sad chronicles of mine.

Somewhere about the beginning of last century appeared at the western corner of Market Street, Sligo, where the butcher's shop now is, not a palace, as in Keats's Lamia, but an apothecary's shop, ruled over by a certain unaccountable Dr Opendon. Where he came from, none ever knew.

There also was in Sligo, in those days, a woman, Ormsby by name, whose husband had fallen mysteriously sick. The doctors could make nothing of him. Nothing seemed wrong with him, yet weaker and weaker he grew. Away went the wife to Dr Opendon. She was shown into the shop parlour. A black cat was sitting straight up before the fire. She had just time to see that the sideboard was covered with fruit, and to say to herself, 'Fruit must be wholesome when the doctor has so much,' before Dr Opendon came in. He was dressed all in black, the same as the cat, and his wife walked behind him dressed in black likewise. She gave him a guinea, and got a little bottle in return. Her husband recovered that time. Meanwhile the black doctor cured many people; but one day a rich patient died, and cat, wife, and doctor all vanished the night after. In a year the man Ormsby fell sick once more. Now he was a good-looking man, and his wife felt sure the 'gentry' were coveting him. She went and called on the 'faery-doctor' at Cairnsfoot. As soon as he heard her tale, he went behind the back door and began muttering, muttering, muttering—making spells. Her husband got well this time also. But after a while he sickened again, the fatal third time, and away went she once more to Cairnsfoot, and out went the faery-doctor behind his back door and began muttering, but soon he came in and told her it was no use—her husband would die; and sure enough the man died, and ever after when she spoke of him Mrs Ormsby shook her head saying she knew well where he was, and it wasn't in heaven or hell or purgatory either. She probably believed that a log of wood was left behind in his place, but so bewitched that it seemed the dead body of her husband.

She is dead now herself, but many still living remember her. She was, I believe, for a time a servant or else a kind of pensioner of some relations of my own.

Sometimes those who are carried off are allowed after many years—seven usually—a final glimpse of their friends. Many years ago a woman vanished suddenly from a Sligo garden where she was walking with her husband. When her son, who was then a baby, had grown up he received word in some way, not handed down, that his mother was glamoured by faeries, and imprisoned for a time in a house in Glasgow and longing to see him. Glasgow in those days of sailing-ships seemed to the peasant mind almost over the edge of the known world, yet he, being a dutiful son, started away. For a long time he walked the streets of Glasgow; at last down in a cellar he saw his mother working. She was happy, she said, and had the best of good eating, and would he not eat? and therewith laid all kinds of food on the table; but he, knowing well that she was trying to cast on him the glamour by giving him faery food, that she might keep him with her, refused and came home to his people in Sligo.

Some five miles southward of Sligo is a gloomy and tree-bordered pond, a great gathering-place of water-fowl, called, because of its form, the Heart Lake. It is haunted by stranger things than heron, snipe, or wild duck. Out of this lake, as from the white square stone in Ben Bulben, issues an unearthly troop. Once men began to drain it; suddenly one of them raised a cry that he saw his house in flames. They turned round, and every man there saw his own cottage burning. They hurried home to find it was but faery glamour. To this hour on the border of the lake is shown a half-dug trench— the signet of their impiety. A little way from this lake I heard a beautiful and mournful history of faery kidnapping. I heard it from a little old woman in a white cap, who sings to herself in Gaelic, and moves from one foot to the other as though she remembered the dancing of her youth.

A young man going at nightfall to the house of his just-married bride, met in the way a jolly company, and with them his bride. They were faeries, and had stolen her as a wife for the chief of their band. To him they seemed only a company of merry mortals. His bride, when she saw her old love, bade him welcome, but was most fearful lest he should eat the faery food, and so be glamoured out of the earth into that bloodless dim nation, wherefore she sat him down to play cards with three of the cavalcade; and he played on, realizing nothing until he saw the chief of the band carrying his bride away in his arms. Immediately he started up, and knew they were faeries; for slowly all that jolly company melted into shadow and night. He returned to the house of his beloved. As he drew near came to him the cry of the keeners. She had died some time before he came. Some noteless Gaelic poet had made this into a forgotten ballad, some odd verses of which my white-capped friend remembered and sang for me.

Sometimes one hears of stolen people acting as good genii to the living, as in this tale, heard also close by the haunted pond, of John Kirwan of Castle Hacket. The Kirwans are a family much rumoured of in peasant stories, and believed to be the descendants of a man and a spirit. They have ever been famous for beauty, and I have read that the mother of the present Lord Cloncurry was of their tribe.

John Kirwan was a great horse-racing man, and once landed in Liverpool with a fine horse, going racing somewhere in middle England. That evening as he walked by the docks, a slip of a boy came up and asked where he was stabling his horse. In such and such a place, he answered. 'Don't put him there,' said the slip of a boy; 'that stable will be burnt to-night.' He took his horse elsewhere, and sure enough the stable was burnt down. Next day the boy came and asked as a reward to ride as his jockey in the coming race, and then was gone. The race-time came round. At the last moment the boy ran forward and mounted, saying, 'If I strike him with the whip in my left hand I will lose, but if in my right hand bet all you are worth.' For, said Paddy Flynn, who told me the tale, 'the left arm is good for nothing. I might go on making the sign of the cross with it and all that, come Christmas, and a Banshee, or such like, would no more mind than if it was that broom.' Well, the slip of a boy struck the horse with his right hand, and John Kirwan cleared the field out. When the race was over, 'What can I do for you now?' said he. 'Nothing but this,' said the boy: 'my mother has a cottage on your land -- they stole me from the cradle. Be good to her, John Kirwan, and wherever your horses go I will watch that no ill follows them; but you will never see me more.' With that he made himself air, and vanished.

Sometimes animals are carried off—apparently drowned animals more than others. In Claremorris, Galway, Paddy Flynn told me, lived a poor widow with one cow and its calf. The cow fell into the river, and was washed away. There was a man thereabouts who went to a red-haired woman— for such are supposed to be wise in these things—and she told him to take the calf down to the edge of the river, and hide himself and watch. He did as she had told him, and as evening came on the calf began to low, and after a while the cow came along the edge of the river and commenced suckling it. Then, as he had been told, he caught the cow's tail. Away they went at a great pace, across hedges and ditches, till they came to a royalty (a name for the circular ditches, commonly called raths or forts, that Ireland is covered with since Pagan times). Therein he saw walking or sitting all the people who had died out of his village in his time. A woman was sitting on the edge with a child on her knees, and she called out to him to mind what the red-haired woman had told him, and he remembered she had said, Bleed the cow. So he stuck his knife into the cow and drew blood. That broke the spell, and he was able to turn her homeward. 'Do not forget the spancel,' said the woman with the child on her knees; 'take the inside one.' There were three spancels on a bush; he took one, and the cow was driven safely home to the widow.

There is hardly a valley or mountain-side where folk cannot tell you of someone pillaged from amongst them. Two or three miles from the Heart Lake lives an old woman who was stolen away in her youth. After seven years she was brought home again for some reason or other, but she had no toes left. She had danced them off. Many near the white stone door in Ben Bulben have been stolen away.

It is far easier to be sensible in cities than in many country places I could tell you of. When one walks on those grey roads at evening by the scented elder-bushes of the white cottages, watching the faint mountains gathering the clouds upon their heads, one all too readily discovers beyond the thin cobweb veil of the sense, those creatures, the goblins, hurrying from the white square stone door to the north, or from the Heart Lake in the south.

Frank Martin and the Fairies

William Carleton

Martin was a thin, pale man, when I saw him, of a sickly look, and a constitution naturally feeble. His hair was a light auburn, his beard mostly unshaven, and his hands of a singular delicacy and whiteness, owing, I dare say, as much to the soft and easy nature of his employment as to his infirm health. In everything else, he was as sensible, sober, and rational as any other man; but on the topic of fairies, the man's mania was peculiarly strong and immovable. Indeed, I remember that the expression of his eyes was singularly wild and hollow, and his long narrow temples sallow and emaciated.

Now, this man did not lead an unhappy life, nor did the malady he laboured under seem to be productive of either pain or terror to him, although one might be apt to imagine otherwise. On the contrary, he and the fairies maintained the most friendly intimacy, and their dialogues—which I fear were woefully one-sided ones—must have been a source of great pleasure to him, for they were conducted with much mirth and laughter, on his part at least.

"Well, Frank, when did you see the fairies?"

"Whist! there's two dozen of them in the shop (the weaving shop) this minute. There's a little ould fellow sittin'on the top of the sleys, an' all to be rocked while I'm weavin'. The sorrow's in them, but they're the greatest little skamers alive, so they are. See, there's another of them at my dressin' nog-gin.* Go out o' that, you shingawn; or, bad cess to me, if you don't, but I'll lave you a mark. Ha! cut, you thief you!"

"Frank, arn't you afeard o' them?"

"Is it me!Arra, what ud' I be afeard o' them for? Sure they have no power over me."

"And why haven't they, Frank?"

"Because I was baptised against them."

"What do you mean by that?"

"Why, the priest that christened me was tould by my

---

*The dressings are a species of sizy flummery, which is brushed into the yarn to keep the thread round and even, and to prevent it from being frayed by the friction of the reed.

father, to put in the proper prayer against the fairies—an' a priest can't refuse it when he's asked—an' he did it so. Begorra, it's well for me that he did—(let the tallow alone, you little glutton—see, there's a weeny thief o' them aitin' my tallow)—becaise, you see, it was their intention to make me king o' the fairies."

"Is it possible?"

"Devil a lie in it. Sure you may ax them, an' they'll tell you."

"What size are they, Frank?"

"Oh, little wee fellows, with green coats, an' the purtiest little shoes ever you seen. There's two of them—both ould acquaintances o' mine—runnin' along the yarn-beam. That ould fellow with the bob-wig is called Jim Jam an' the other chap, with the three-cocked hat, is called Nickey Nick. Nickey plays the pipes. Nickey, give us a tune, or I'll malivogue you—come now, 'Lough Erne Shore'. Whist, now—listen!"

The poor fellow, though weaving as fast as he could all the time, yet bestowed every possible mark of attention to the music, and seemed to enjoy it as much as if it had been real.

But who can tell whether that which we look upon as a privation may not after all be a fountain of increased happiness, greater, perhaps, than any which we ourselves enjoy? I forget who the poet is who says—

"Mysterious are thy laws;
The vision's finer than the view;
Her landscape Nature never drew
So fair as Fancy draws."

Many a time, when a mere child, not more than six or seven years of age, have I gone as far as Frank's weaving-shop, in order, with a heart divided between curiosity and fear, to listen to his conversation with the good people. From morning till night his tongue was going almost as incessantly as his shuttle; and it was well known that at night, whenever he awoke out of his sleep, the first thing he did was to put out his hand, and push them, as it were, off his bed.

"Go out o' this, you thieves, you—go out o' this now, an' let me alone. Nickey, is this any time to be playing the pipes, and me wants to sleep? Go off, now—troth if yez do, you'll see what I'll give yez tomorrow. Sure I'll be makin' new dressin's; and if yez behave decently, maybe I'll lave yez the scrapin' o' the pot. There now. Och! poor things, they're dacent crathurs. Sure they're all gone, barrin' poor Red-cap, that doesn't like to lave me." And then the harmless monomaniac would fall back into what we trust was an innocent slumber.

About this time there was said to have occurred a very remarkable circumstance, which gave poor Frank a vast deal of importance among the neighbours. A man named Frank

Thomas, the same in whose house Mickey M'Rorey held the first dance at which I ever saw him, as detailed in a former sketch; this man, I say, had a child sick, but of what complaint I cannot now remember, nor is it of any importance. One of the gables of Thomas's house was built against, or rather into, a Forth or Rath, called Towny, or properly Tonagh Forth. It was said to be haunted by the fairies, and what gave it a character peculiarly wild in my eyes was, that there were on the southern side of it two or three little green mounds, which were said to be the graves of unchristened children, over which it was considered dangerous and unlucky to pass. At all events, the season was mid-summer; and one evening about dusk, during the illness of the child, the noise of a hand-saw was heard upon the Forth. This was considered rather strange, and, after a little time, a few of those who were assembled at Frank Thomas's went to see who it could be that was sawing in such a place, or what they could be sawing at so late an hour, for every one knew that nobody in the whole country about them would dare to cut down the few white-thorns that grew upon the Forth. On going to examine, however, judge of their surprise, when, after surrounding and searching the whole place, they could discover no trace of either saw or sawyer. In fact, with the exception of themselves, there was no one, either natural or supernatural, visible. They then returned to the house, and had scarcely sat down, when it was heard again within ten yards of them. Another examination of the premises took place, but with equal success. Now, however, while standing on the Forth, they heard the sawing in a little hollow, about a hundred and fifty yards below them, which was completely exposed to their view, but they could see nobody. A party of them immediately went down to ascertain, if possible, what this singular noise and invisible labor could mean; but on arriving at the spot, they heard the sawing, to which were now added hammering, and the driving of nails upon the Forth above, whilst those who stood on the Forth continued to hear it in the hollow. On comparing notes, they resolved to send down to Billy Nelson's for Frank Martin, a distance of only about eighty or ninety yards. He was soon on the spot, and without a moment's hesitation solved the enigma.

"'Tis the fairies," said he. "I see them, and busy crathurs they are."

"But what are they sawing, Frank?"

"They are making a child's coffin," he replied; "they have the body already made, an' they're now nailin' the lid together."

That night the child died, and the story goes that on the second evening afterwards, the carpenter who was called upon to make the coffin brought a table out from Thomas's house to the Forth, as a temporary bench; and, it is said, that the sawing and hammering necessary for the completion of his task were precisely the same which had been heard the evening but one before—neither more nor less. I remember the death of the child myself, and the making of its coffin, but I think the story of the supernatural carpenter was not heard in the village for some months after its interment.

Frank had every appearance of a hypochondriac about him. At the time I saw him, he might be about thirty-four years of age, but I do not think, from the debility of his frame and inform health, that he has been alive for several years. He was an object of considerable interest and curiosity, and often have I been present when he was pointed out to strangers as "the man that could see the good people."

The Piper and the Puca

Douglas Hyde

In the old times, there was a half fool living in Dunmore, in the county Galway, and although he was excessively fond of music, he was unable to learn more than one tune, and that was the "Black Rogue". He used to get a good deal of money from the gentlemen, for they used to get sport out of him. One night the piper was coming home from a house where there had been a dance, and he half drunk. When he came to a little bridge that was up by his mother's house, he squeezed the pipes on, and began playing the "Black Rogue" (*an rogaire dugh*). The Puca came behind him, and flung him up on his own back. There were long horns of the

Translated literally from the Irish of the Leabhar Sgeulaigheachta.

Puca, and the piper got a good rip of them, and then he said—
"Destruction on you, you nasty beast, let me home. I have a
ten-penny piece in my pocket for my mother, and she wants
snuff."

"Never mind your mother," said the Puca, "but keep
your hold. If you fall, you will break your neck and your pipes."
Then the Puca said to him, "Play up for me the `Shan Van
Vocht' (*an t-seann-bhean bhocht*)."

"I don't know it," said the piper.

"Never mind whether you do or you don't," said the
Puca. "Play up, and I'll make you know."

The piper put wind in his bag, and he played such
music as made himself wonder.

"Upon my word, you're a fine music-master," says the
piper then; "but tell me where you're for bringing me."

"There's a great feast in the house of the Banshee, on
the top of Croagh Patric tonight," says the Puca, "and I'm for
bringing you there to play music, and, take my word, you'll get
the price of your trouble."

"By my word, you'll save me a journey, then," says the
piper, "for Father William put a journey to Croagh Patric on
me, because I stole the white gander from him last
Martinmas."

The Puca rushed him across hills and bogs and rough
places, till he brought him to the top of Croagh Patric. Then the

Puca struck three blows with his foot, and a great door opened, and they passed in together, into a fine room.

The piper saw a golden table in the middle of the room, and hundreds of old women (*cailleacha*) sitting around it. The old woman rose up, and said, "A hundred thousand welcomes to you, you Puca of November (*na Samhna*). Who is this you have brought with you?"

"The best piper in Ireland," says the Puca.

One of the old women struck a blow on the ground, and a door opened in the side of the wall, and what should the piper see coming out but the white gander which he had stolen from Father William.

"By my conscience, then," says the piper, "myself and my mother ate every taste of that gander, only one wing, and I gave that to *Moy-rua* (Red Mary), and it's she told the priest I stole his gander."

The gander cleaned the table, and carried it away, and the Puca said, "Play up music for these ladies."

The piper played up, and the old women began dancing, and they were dancing till they were tired. Then the Puca said to pay the piper, and every old woman drew out a gold piece, and gave it to him.

"By the tooth of Patric," said he, "I'm as rich as the son of a lord."

"Come with me," says the Puca, "and I'll bring you home."

They went out then, and just as he was going to ride on the Puca, the gander came up to him, and gave him a new set of pipes. The Puca was not long until he brought him to Dunmore, and he threw the piper off at the little bridge, and then he told him to go home, and says to him, "You have two things now that you never had before— you have sense and music (*ciall agus ceol*).

The piper went home, and he knocked at his mother's door, saying, "Let me in, I'm as rich as a lord, and I'm the best piper in Ireland."

"You're drunk," said the mother.

"No, indeed," says the piper, "I haven't drunk a drop."

The mother let him in, and he gave her the gold pieces, and, "Wait now," says he, "till you hear the music, I'll play."

He buckled on the pipes, but instead of music, there came a sound as if all the geese in Ireland were screeching together. He awakened the neighbours and they all were mocking him, until he put on the old pipes, and then he played melodious music for them; and after that he told them all he had gone through the night.

The next morning, when his mother went to look at the gold pieces, there was nothing there but the leaves of a plant.

The piper went to the priest, and told him his story, but the priest would not believe a word from him, until he put the pipes on him, and then the screeching of the ganders and geese began.

"Leave my sight, you thief," said the priest.

But nothing would do the piper till he would put the old pipes on him to show the priest that his story was true.

He buckled on the old pipes, and he played melodious music, and from that day till the day of his death, there was never a piper in the county Galway was as good as he was.

A Donegal Fairy
Letitia Maclintock

Ay, it's a bad thing to displeasure the gentry, sure enough—they can be unfriendly if they're angered, an' they can be the very best o' gude neighbours if they're treated kindly.

My mother's sister was her lone in the house one day, wi' a big pot o' water boiling on the fire, and ane o' the wee folk fell down the chimney, and slipped wi' his leg in the hot water.

He let a terrible squeal out o' him, an' in a minute the house was full o' wee crathurs pulling him out o' the pot, an' carrying him across the floor.

"Did she scald you?" my aunt heard them saying to him.

"Na, na, it was mysel' scalded my ainsel'," quoth the wee fellow.

"A weel, a weel," says they. "If it was your ainsel scalded yoursel', we'll say nothing, but if she had scalded you, we'd ha' made her pay."

Drumcliff and Rosses
William Butler Yeats

Drumcliff and Rosses were, are, and ever shall be, please Heaven! places of unearthly resort. I have lived near by them and in them, time after time, and have gathered thus many a crumb of faery lore. Drumcliff is a wide green valley, lying at the foot of Ben Bulben, the mountain in whose side the square white door swings open at nightfall to loose the faery riders on the world. The great St Columba himself, the builder of many of the old ruins in the valley, climbed the mountains on one notable day to get near heaven with his prayers. Rosses is a little sea-dividing, sandy plain, covered with short grass, like a green tablecloth, and lying in the foam midway between the round cairn-headed Knocknarea and 'Ben Bulben, famous for hawks':

'But for Benbulben and Knocknarea
Many a poor sailor'd be cast away.'
as the rhyme goes.

At the northern corner of Rosses is a little promontory of sand and rocks and grass: a mournful, haunted place. No wise peasant would fall asleep under its low cliff, for he who sleeps here may wake 'silly,' the 'good people' having carried off his soul. There is no more ready short-cut to the dim kingdom than this plovery headland, for, covered and smothered now from sight by mounds of sand, a long cave goes thither 'full of gold and silver, and the most beautiful parlours and drawing-rooms.' Once, before the sand covered it, a dog strayed in, and was heard yelping helplessly deep underground in a fort far inland. These forts or raths, made before modern history had begun, cover all Rosses and all Columkille. The one where the dog yelped has, like most others, an underground beehive chamber in the midst. Once when I was poking about there, an unusually intelligent and 'reading' peasant who had come with me, and waited outside, knelt down by the opening, and whispered in a timid voice, 'Are you all right, sir?' I had been some little while underground, and he feared I had been carried off like the dog.

No wonder he was afraid, for the fort has long been circled by ill-boding rumours. It is on the ridge of a small hill, on whose northern slope lie a few stray cottages. One night a farmer's young son came from one of them and saw the fort all flaming, and ran towards it, but the 'glamour' fell on him, and he sprang on to a fence, cross-legged, and commenced beating it with a stick, for he imagined the fence was a horse, and that all night long he went on the most wonderful ride through the country. In the morning he was still beating his fence, and they carried him home, where he remained a simpleton for three years before he came to himself again. A little later a farmer tried to level the fort. His cows and horses died, and all manner of trouble overtook him, and finally he himself was led home, and left useless with 'his head on his knees by the fire to the day of his death.'

A few hundred yards southwards of the northern angle of Rosses is another angle having also its cave, though this one is not covered with sand. About twenty years ago a brig was wrecked near by, and three or four fishermen were put to watch the deserted hulk through the darkness. At midnight they saw sitting on a stone at the cave's mouth two red-capped fiddlers fiddling with all their might. The men fled. A great crowd of villagers rushed down to the cave to see the fiddlers but the creatures had gone.

To the wise peasant the green hills and woods round him are full of never-fading mystery. When the aged country-woman stands at her door in the evening, and in her own words, 'looks at the mountains and thinks of the goodness of

God,' God is all the nearer, because the pagan powers are not far: because northward in Ben Bulben, famous for hawks, the white square door swings open at sundown, and those wild unchristian riders rush forth upon the fields, while southward the White Lady, who is doubtless Maive herself, wanders under the broad cloud nightcap of Knocknarea. How may she doubt these things, even though the priest shakes his head at her? Did not a herd-boy, no long while since, see the White Lady? She passed so close that the skirt of her dress touched him. 'He fell down, and was dead three days.' But this is merely the small gossip of faerydom—the little stitches that join this world and the other.

One night as I sat eating Mrs H—'s soda-bread, her husband told me a longish story, much the best of all I heard in Rosses. Many a poor man from Fin M'Cool to our own days has had some such adventure to tell of, for those creatures, the 'good people,' love to repeat themselves. At any rate the story-tellers do. 'In the times when we used to travel by the canal,' he said, 'I was coming down from Dublin. When we came to Mullingar the canal ended, and I began to walk, and stiff and fatigued I was after the slowness. I had some friends with me, and now and then we walked, now and then we rode in a car. So on till we saw some girls milking cows, and stopped to joke with them. After a while we asked them for a drink of milk. "We have nothing to put it in here," they said, "but come to the house with us." We went home with them, and sat round the fire talking. After a while the others went, and left me, loath to stir from the good fire. I asked the girls for something to et. There was a pot on the fire, and they took the meat out and put it on a plate, and told me to eat only the meat that came off the head. When I had eaten, the girls went out, and I did not see them again. It grew darker and darker, and there I still sat, loath as ever to leave the good fire, and after a while two men came in, carrying between them a corpse. When I saw them coming in I hid behind the door. Says one to the other, putting the corpse on the spit, "Who'll turn the spit?" Says the other, "Michael H—, come out of that and turn the meat." I came out all of a tremble, and began turning the spit. "Michael H—," says the one who spoke first," if you let it burn we'll have to put you on the spit instead"; and on that they went out. I sat there trembling and turning the corpse till towards midnight. The men came again, and the one said it was burnt, and the other said it was done right. But having fallen out over it, they both said they would do me no harm that time; and, sitting by the fire, one of them cried out: "Michael H—, can you tell me a story?" "Divil a one," said I. On which he caught me by the shoulder, and put me out like a shot. It was a wild blowing night. Never in all my born days did I see such a night—the darkest night that ever came of the heavens. I did not know where I was for the life of me. So when one of the men came after me and touched me on the shoulder, with a "Michael H—, can you tell a story now?" "I can," says I. In he brought me; and putting me by the fire, says: "Begin." "I have no story but the one," says I, "that I was sitting here, and you two men brought in a corpse and put it on the spit and set me turning it." "That will do," says he; "ye may go in there and lie down on the bed." And I went, nothing loath; and in the morning where was I but in the middle of a green field!

'Drumcliff' is a great place for omens. Before a prosperous fishing season a herring-barrel appears in the midst of a storm-cloud; and at a place called Columkille's Strand, a place of march and mire, an ancient boat, with St Columba himself, comes floating in from the sea on a moonlight night; a portent of a brave harvesting. They have their dread portents too. Some few seasons ago a fisherman saw, far on the horizon, renowned Hy Brazel, where he who touches shall find no more labour or care, nor cynic laughter, but shall go walking about under shadiest boscage, and enjoy the conversation of Cuchulain and his heroes. A vision of Hy Brazel forebodes national troubles.

Drumcliff and Rosses are chokefull of ghosts. By bog, road, rath, hillside, sea-border they gather in all shapes: headless women, men in armour, shadow-hares, fire-tongued hounds, whistling seals, and so on. A whistling seal sank a ship the other day. At Drumcliff there is a very ancient grave-yard. The Annals of the Four Masters have this verse about a soldier named Denadhach, who died in 871: 'A pious soldier of the race of Con lies under hazel crosses at Drumcliff.' Not very long ago an old woman, turning to go into the churchyard at night to pray, saw standing before her a man in armour, who asked her where she was going. It was the 'pious soldier of the race of Con,' says local wisdom, still keeping watch, with his ancient piety, over the graveyard. Again, the custom is still common hereabouts of sprinkling the doorstep with the blood of a chicken on the death of a very young child, thus (as belief is) drawing into the blood the evil spirits from the too weak soul. Blood is a great gatherer of evil spirits. To cut your hand on a stone on going into a fort is said to be very dangerous.

There is no more curious ghost in Drumcliff or Rosses than the snipe-ghost. There is a bush behind a house in a village that I know well: for excellent reasons I do not say whether in Drumcliff or Rosses or on the slope of Ben Bulben, or even on the plain round Knocknarea. There is a history concerning the house and the bush. A man once lived there who found on the quay of Sligo a package containing three hundred pounds in notes. It was dropped by a foreign sea captain. This my man knew, but said nothing. It was money for freight, and the sea captain, not daring to face the owners, committed suicide in mid-ocean. Shortly afterwards my man died. His soul could not rest. At any rate, strange sounds were heard round his house, though that had grown and prospered since the freight money. The wife was often seen by those still alive out in the garden praying at the bush I have spoken of, for the shade of the dead man appeared there at times. The bush remains to this day: once portion of a hedge, it now stands by itself, for no one dare put spade or pruning-knife about it. As to the strange sounds and voices, they did not cease till a few years ago, when, during some repairs, a snipe flew out of the solid plaster and away; the troubled ghost, say the neighbours, of the note-finder was at last dislodged.

My forebears and relations have lived near Rosses and Drumcliff these many years. A few miles northward I am wholly a stranger, and can find nothing. When I ask for stories of the faeries, my answer is some such as was given me by a woman who lives near a white stone fort—one of the few stone ones in Ireland—under the seaward angle of Ben Bulben: "They always mind their own affairs and I always mind mine': for it is dangerous to talk of the creatures. Only friendship for yourself or knowledge of your forebears will loosen these cautious tongues. My friend, 'the sweet Harp-String" (I give no more than his Irish name for fear of gaugers), has the science of unpacking the stubbornest heart, but then he supplies the potheen-makers with grain from his own fields. Besides, he is descended from a noted Gaelic magician who raised the 'dhoul' in Great Eliza's century, and he has a kind of prescriptive right to hear tell of all kind of other-world creatures. They are almost relations of his, if all people say concerning the parentage of magicians be true.

The Legend of Knockfierna

T. Crofton Croker

It is a very good thing not to be any way in dread of the fairies, for without doubt they have then less power over a person, but to make too free with them, or to disbelieve in them altogether, is as foolish a thing as man, woman, or child can do.

It has been truly said that "good manners are no burthen," and that "civility costs nothing, "but there are some people foolhardy enough to disregard doing a civil thing, which, whatever they may think, can never harm themselves or anyone else, and who, at the same time, will go out of their way for a bit of mischief which never can serve them. But sooner or later they will come to know better, as you shall hear of Carroll O'Daly, a strapping young fellow up out of Connacht, whom they used to call in his own country "Devil Daly."

Carroll O'Daly used to go roving about from one place to another, and the fear of nothing stopped him. He would as soon pass an old churchyard, or a regular fairy ground, at any hour of the night, as go from one room into another, without ever making the sign of the cross, or saying, "Good luck attend you, gentlemen."

It so happened that he was once journeying in the County of Limerick, towards, "the Balbec of Ireland," the venerable town of Kilmallock, and just at the foot of Knockfierna he overtook a respectable-looking man jogging along upon a white pony. The night was coming on, and they rode side by side for some time, without much conversation passing between them, further than saluting each other very kindly. At last, Carroll O'Daly asked his companion how far he was going.

"Not far your way," said the farmer, for such his appearance bespoke him. "I'm only going to the top of this hill here."

"And what might take you there," said O'Daly, "at this time of the night?"

"Why then," replied the farmer, "if you want to know, 'tis the good people."

"The fairies, you mean," said O'Daly.

"Whist! whist!" said his fellow-traveler, "or you may be sorry for it," and he turned his pony off the road they were going, towards a little path which led up the side of the mountain, wishing Carroll O'Daly good night and a safe journey.

"That fellow," thought Carroll, "is about no good this blessed night, and I would have no fear of swearing wrong if I took my Bible oath, that it is something else beside the fairies, or the Good People, as he calls them, that is taking him up the mountain at this hour. The fairies!" he repeated. "Is it for a well-shaped man like him to going after little chaps like the fairies? To be sure some say there are such things, and more say not. But I know this, that never afraid would I be of a dozen of them—aye of two dozen for that matter, if they are no bigger than what I hear tell of."

Carroll O'Daly, whilst these thoughts were passing in his mind, had fixed his eyes steadfastly on the mountain, behind which the full moon was rising majestically. Upon an elevated point that appeared darkly against the moon's disk, he beheld the figure of a man leading a pony, and he had no doubt it was that of the farmer with whom he had just parted company.

A sudden resolve to follow flashed across the mind of O'Daly with the speed of lightning: both his courage and curiosity had been worked up by his cogitations to a pitch of

chivalry, and muttering; "Here's after you, old boy," he dismounted from his horse, bound him to an old thorn-tree, and
then commenced vigourously ascending the mountain.

Following as well as he could the direction taken by
the figures of the man and pony, he pursued his way, occasionally guided by their partial appearance; and after toiling
nearly three hours over a rugged and sometimes swampy
path, came to a green spot on the top of the mountain, where
he saw the white pony at full liberty grazing as quietly as may
be. O'Daly looked around for the rider, but he was nowhere to
be seen; he, however, soon discovered, close to where the
pony stood, an opening in the mountain like the mouth of a
pit, and he remembered having heard, when a child, many a
tale about the "Poul-duve," or Black Hole, of Knockfierna; how
it was the entrance to the fairy castle which was within the
mountain; and how a man whose name was Ahern, a land
surveyor in that part of the country, had once attempted to
fathom it with a line, and had been drawn down into it and
was never again heard of; with many other tales of like nature.

"But," thought O'Daly, "these are old women's stories;
and since I've come up so far I'll just knock at the castle door,
and see if the fairies are at home."

No sooner said than done; for, seizing a large stone, as
big, aye, bigger than his two hands, he flung it with all his
strength down into the Poul-duve of Knockfierna. He heard it

bounding and tumbling about from one rock to another with a terrible noise, and he leant his head over to try and hear when it would reach the bottom—and what should the very stone he had thrown in do but come up again with as much force as it had gone down, and gave him such a blow full in the face, that it sent him rolling down the side of Knockfierna, head over heels, tumbling from one crag to another, much faster than he came up. And in the morning Carroll O'Daly was found lying beside his horse; the bridge of his nose broken, which disfigured him for life; his head all cut and bruised, and both his eyes closed up, and as black as if Sir Daniel Donnelly had painted them for him.

Carroll O'Daly was never bold again in riding alone near the haunts of the fairies after dusk; but small blame to him for that, and if ever he happened to be benighted in a lonesome place he would make the best of his way to his journey's end, without asking questions, or turning to the right or to the left, to seek after the good people, or any who kept company with them.

The Four-Leafed Shamrock

Jeremiah Curtin

A good many years ago a showman came to the town of Dingle and performed many tricks there. At one time he'd eat a dozen straws and then pull yards of ribbon from his throat. The strangest thing he showed was a game-cock that he used to harness to a great log of wood.

Men, women, and children were breaking their bones, running to see the cock, and he a small bird, drawing such a great weight of timber. One day, when the showman was driving the cock on the road toward Brandon Mountain, he met a man with a bundle of fresh grass on his back. The man was astonished to see crowds running after a cock dragging one straw behind him.

"You fool," said the people, "don't you see the cock drawing a log of timber, and it would fail any horse to draw the like of it?"

"Indeed, then, I do not. I see the cock dragging a straw behind him, and sure I've seen the like many a time in my own place."

Hearing this, the showman knew that there was something in the grass, and going over to the man he asked what price was he asking for the bundle. The man didn't wish to sell the grass, but at last he parted with it for eighteen pence. The showman gave the grass to his boy and told him to go aside and drop it into the river. The boy did that, and when the bundle went down with the stream the man was as big a fool as another; he ran after the cock with the crowd.

That evening the same man was telling a friend how at first he saw the cock with a straw behind him, and then saw him drawing a great log of wood. "Oh, you fool!" said the friend, "there was a four-leafed shamrock in your bundle of grass, while you had the shamrock it kept every enchantment and devilment from you, and when you parted with it, you became as big a fool as the others."

Paddy Corcoran's Wife

William Carleton

Paddy Corcoran's wife was for several years afflicted with a kind of complaint which nobody could properly understand. She was sick, and she was not sick; she was well, and she was not well; she was as ladies wish to be who love their lords, and she was not as such ladies wish to be. In fact nobody could tell what the matter with her was. She had a gnawing at the heart which came heavily upon her husband; for, with the help of God, a keener appetite than the same gnawing amounted to could not be met with of a summer's day. The poor woman was delicate beyond belief, and had no appetite at all, so she hadn't barring a little relish for a mutton-chop, or a "staik," or a bit o' mait, anyway; for sure, God help her! she hadn't the laist inclination for the dhry pratie, or the dhrop o' sour buttermilk along wid it, especially as she was so poorly; and, indeed, for a woman in her condition—but God's will be done! she didn't care. A pratie an' a grain o' salt was a welcome to her—glory be to his name!—as the best roast an' boiled that ever was dressed; and why not? There was one comfort: she wouldn't be long wid him—long troublin' him; it matthered little what she got; but sure she knew herself, that from the gnawin' at her heart, she could never do good widout the little bit o' mait now and then; an', sure, if her own husband begridged it to her, who else had she a better right to expect it from?

Well, as we have said, she lay a bedridden invalid for long enough, trying doctors and quacks of all sorts, sexes, and sizes, and all without a farthing's benefit, until, at the long run, poor Paddy was nearly brought to the last pass in striving to keep her in "the bit o' mait." The seventh year was now on the point of closing, when, one harvest day, as she lay bemoaning her hard condition, on her bed beyond the kitchen fire, a little weeshy woman, dressed in a neat red cloak, comes in, and sitting down by the hearth, says:

"Well, Kitty Corcoran, you've had a long lair of it there on the broad o' yer back for seven years, an' you're jist as far from bein' cured as ever."

"Mavrone, ay" said the other; "in troth that's what I was

this minnit thinkin' ov, and a sorrowful thought it's to me."

"It's yer own fau't, thin," says the little woman; "an', indeed, for that matter, it's yer fau't that ever you wor there at all."

"Arra, how is that?" asked Kitty; "sure I wouldn't be here if I could help it? Do you think it's a comfort or a pleasure to me to be sick and bedridden?"

"No," said the other, "I do not; but I'll tell you the truth; for the last seven years you have been annoying us. I am one o' the good people; an' as I have a regard for you, I'm come to let you know the raison why you've been sick so long as you are. For all the time you've been ill, if you'll take the thrubble to remimber, your childre threwn out yer dirty wather afther dusk an' before sunrise, at the very time we're passin' yer door, which we pass twice a-day. Now, if you avoid this, if you throw it out in a different place, an' at a different time, the complaint you have will lave you; so will the gnawin' at the heart; an' you'll be as well as ever you wor. If you don't follow this advice, why, remain as you are, an' al the art o' man can't cure you." She then bade her good-bye, and disappeared.

Kitty, who was glad to be cured on such easy terms, immediately complied with the injunction of the fairy; and the consequence was, that the next day she found herself in as good health as ever she enjoyed during her life.

Maurice Griffin the Fairy Doctor

Jeremiah Curtin

There was a man at Dun Lean named Maurice Griffin. He was in service as a herder minding cows, and one morning while out with the cattle he saw something come down through the air in the form of a white cloud and drop on a hillock. It settled to be a lump of white foam, and a great heat rose out of it then. One of the cows went to the hillock and licked the foam till she swallowed every bit of it.

When he went into breakfast Maurice told the man of the house about the cloud, and that it was a wonder to see the cow licking up what had settled on the hillock. "And it was white as any linen," said he.

When the man of the house sent the servant girl to milk the cow that evening he told her not to spill any drop of the milk till she had it brought to himself.

Maurice Griffin went with the girl, caught the cow, and held her. The vessel the girl was milking in did not hold half the milk. She did not like to leave the cow partly milked.

"Drink some of this," said she, "and let me finish, for it would spoil the cow to leave part of the milk with her."

Maurice Griffin emptied the vessel three times, drank all there was in it. The girl filled it the fourth time and went home with the milk. The master asked, "Was any of the milk spilled or used?" She told him truly, "This is the same vessel that I use always in milking, and that cow never filled it before till to-night. I didn't like to leave any milk with her, so I gave some to Maurice."

"It was his luck give him all; 'twas promised to him, not to me," said the master. He was fonder of Maurice Griffin than ever, and Maurice began to foretell right away and cure people. The report went out through the country that all he foretold came to pass, and all he undertook to cure he cured. The priest, hearing this, didn't want to have the like of him in the parish, and spoke of him from the altar, but Griffin gave no answer. One morning the priest went to where Griffin was, saluted him, and was saluted in turn. "I hear that you are curing and foretelling," said the priest. "Where did you get the knowledge to foretell and to cure?"

"I foretell and I cure many persons, I serve people," said Griffin; "and my business is as good as yours. Some say that you have power, your reverence, but if you have, you are not foretelling or curing."

"Well," said the priest, "I'll know can you foretell or not. Answer me a question, and if you can I'll believe you."

"I'll answer you any questions you'll put to me," said Griffin.

"What time or minute of the day did the last new moon appear?"

"I will tell you that," said Griffin. "Do you remember that when you were passing Travug your horse stooped to drink and his right leg was first in the river? Under your neck you wear a stone which the Pope gave you; this stone always sweats three drops at the new moon; the stone sweated three drops when the horse's right foot touched the water, and that was the time of the new moon."

"Oh," said the priest, "what is rumoured of you is true; follow your hand, I'll not meddle with you from this out."

Griffin came home then and told the conversation. The master grew very fond of him after that, and having an only daughter he gave her to Maurice, and Griffin lived with his father-in-law till the old man died and left all he had to his son-in-law.

The people thought a deal of Griffin when he got the property, and they came for counsel and cure to him.

Griffin had two sons; in course of time he grew old and at last was very weak, and his first son, Dyeermud, managed the property. In those days everything was carried to Cork on horseback. Griffin called Dyeermud one day to him and said, "I am in dread that I am going to die. I don't want you to go to Cork to be absent so long."

"The company is going, and I'd like to go, too," said Dyeermud. "My brother is here; he will care for you and attend to everything while I am gone."

"I want you here," said the father, "for it's to you I will do all the good."

Dyeermud had a great wish to visit Cork. "Go," said the father, "but you'll be the loser, and you'll remember my words."

Dyeermud went to Cork, and during his absence the father became very sick. Once, when the younger son was sitting at his bedside, the old man said, "I am in dread your brother will not be at home."

"What you were to leave him leave me," said the son.

"I cannot. I'll give you the gift of curing, but foretelling I could not give if I wished."

"How can you give the gift of curing?"

"I'll give it to you," said the father. "Go out tonight, kill a sheep and dress it, pick the right shoulder as clean as any bone could be cleaned from flesh, and in the night look over that bone, and the third time you look you'll see every one that you knew who is dead. Keep that bone with you always and sleep with it, and what you want to know to cure any disease will come to you from the bone. When a person is to be cured from a fairy stroke, look over the bone and a messenger will come from the fairies, and you will be able to cure those who come to you."

"As you will not give me the knowledge of foretelling, I will not take the curing. I will live honestly."

"I have no power to give you the knowledge ," said the father, "but since you will not take the curing I will give it to your mother. The knowledge I can give to no one but your elder brother."

Griffin gave the curing to the wife. The knowledge he could give to no one but the elder son, and to him only if present.

Maurice Griffin died and was buried before Dyeermud came from Cork.

Dyeermud was astonished when he came and didn't find the father.

"You did badly not to stay," said the younger brother.

"Didn't I leave you?"

"You did, but he could leave the knowledge only to you."

"Why didn't he give you the curing?"

"He offered it to me, but I thought it too much trouble. I

would use it if I had it. I let it go to our mother. She is old; let her have it. As he did not give me the knowledge I didn't want the curing. Maybe in after years when I have children it's on them the diseases I cured would come."

It was rumoured that the curing was with the mother, and the people were coming to her.

Once her godson got a fairy stroke in the leg, and she was vexed because his parents did not bring him quickly, for next day she would not be able to cure him at all. At last they came, and she was angry that they were so slow.

"You might have made bacon of him if you waited till morning," cried she. She cured him, and he was a very strong boy after that.

The parish priest had a sick horse left out to die. The clerk was very sorry, the horse was such a fine beast. "Wouldn't it be better to go to Mrs. Griffin?" asked he.

"Oh, how could she cure the horse?" asked the priest.

"I'll go to her," said the clerk.

"If you go to her," said the priest, "I give you no leave."

The clerk went, told Mrs. Griffin that he had come in spite of the priest, and to cure the horse if she could. "It was the priest himself that injured the horse," said Mrs. Griffin. "He gave him water while hot from driving, and because the priest is fond of the horse he patted him and muttered something without saying God bless you. Go now, spit three times into the horse's ears, and say God bless you."

The clerk went and did this; the horse rose up as well and sound as ever, and the clerk brought him to the stable. The priest was astonished, and said, "They have a gift in the family: I'll not trouble them any turn again."

Mrs. Griffin was not able to give her gift to any one; the bone was buried with her.

When he had finished this story Malone said that there were different kinds of doctors, but that all received their power either through inheritance, "it was in the family," or by a sudden gift.

Herb doctors are in much esteem among country people, and gain their knowledge from supernatural sources. They don't learn: "it is given to them." The following are two cases cited by the old man.

In former times all the people had great faith in old women who were herb doctors. These women became doctors, not by learning difficult herbs, and studying, but by a supernatural power, and this power came to them always without their expecting it.

One women of great name as a doctor got her power in this way. Three women were going to a village a mile out of Dingle. On the road they came to a small river, and there was no way to cross, but to walk through the water. All at once a fine lady stood before them, spoke very kindly to the first woman, and asked would she carry her over the river.

"Indeed, then, I will not; I've enough to do to carry myself."

The lady asked the second woman and received a like answer, but when the third woman was asked she said:

"I will carry you and welcome, and why not?" So she took the fine lady on her back, carried her over the water, and put her down on the dry bank.

The lady thanked her very kindly, and said, "When you wake to-morrow morning you will know all plants and herbs, you will know what their names are, and what virtues are in them."

Next morning when the woman woke she could call all plants and herbs by name, she knew where they grew, and knew the power of each, from that out she was a great doctor.

Sometimes the best doctors will leave off curing, for they say that curing will bring misfortune in the end to the doctors or their children. It is believed firmly that there is a compensation for all this supernatural knowledge, and for everything out of the usual course of things. All the people believe that priests have the power of curing if they would only use it, but they are unwilling to take on themselves the punishment for curing. In former days they took pity on poor people sometimes and risked their health to cure them.

St. Martin's Eve

Jeremiah Curtin

In Iveragh, not very far from the town of Cahirciveen, there lived a farmer named James Shea with his wife and three children, two sons and a daughter. The man was peaceable, honest, and very charitable to the poor, but his wife was hard-hearted, never giving even a drink of milk to a needy person. Her younger son was as bad in every way as herself, and whatever the mother did he always agreed with her and was on her side.

This was before the roads and cars were in the Kerry Mountains. The only way of travelling in those days, when a man didn't walk, was to ride sitting on a straw saddle, and the

Told to Jeremiah Curtin by John Sheehy.

only way to take anything to market was on horseback in creels.

It happened, at any rate, that James Shea was going in the beginning of November to Cork with two firkins of butter, and what troubled him most was the fear that he'd not be home on Saint Martin's night to do honour to the saint. For never had he let that night pass without drawing blood in honour of the saint. To make sure, he called the eldest son and said, "if I am not at the house on Saint Martin's night, kill the big sheep that is running with the cows."

Shea went away to Cork with the butter, but could not be home in time. The elder son went out on Saint Martin's eve, when he saw that his father was not coming, and drove the sheep into the house.

"What are you doing, you fool, with that sheep?" asked the mother.

"Sure, I'm going to kill it. Didn't you hear my father tell me that there was never a Saint Martin's night but he drew blood, and do you want to have the house disgraced?"

At this the mother made sport of him and said; "Drive out the sheep and I'll give you something else to kill by and by." So the boy let the sheep out, thinking the mother would kill a goose.

He sat down and waited for the mother to give him whatever she had to kill. It wasn't long till she came in, bringing a big tomcat they had, and the same cat was in the house nine or ten years.

"Here," said she, "you can kill this beast and draw its blood. We'll have it cooked when your father comes home."

The boy was very angry and spoke up to the mother: "Sure the house is disgraced for ever," said he, "and it will not be easy for you to satisfy my father when he comes."

He didn't kill the cat, you may be sure; and neither he nor his sister ate a bite of supper, and they were crying and fretting over the disgrace all the evening.

That very night the house caught fire and burned down, nothing was left but the four walls. The mother and younger son were burned to death, but the elder son and his sister escaped by some miracle. They went to a neighbour's house, and were still there till the father came on the following evening. When he found the house destroyed and the wife and younger son dead he mourned and lamented. But when the other son told him what the mother did on Saint Martin's eve, he cried out:

"Ah, it was the wrath of God that fell on my house; if I had stopped at home till after Saint Martin's night, all would be safe and well with me now."

James Shea went to the priest on the following morning, and asked would it be good or lucky for him to rebuild the house.

"Indeed," said the priest, "there is no harm in putting a roof on the walls and repairing them if you will have Mass celebrated in the house before you go to live in it. If you do that all will be well with you."

[Shea spoke to the priest because people are opposed to repairing or rebuilding a burnt house, and especially if any person has been burned in it.]

Well, James Shea put a roof on the house, repaired it, and had Mass celebrated inside. That evening as Shea was sitting down to supper what should he see but his wife coming in the door to him. He thought she wasn't dead at all. "Ah, Mary," said he, "'tis not so bad as they told me. Sure, I thought it is dead you were. Oh, then you are welcome home; come and sit down here; the supper is just ready."

She didn't answer a word, but looked him straight in the face and walked on to the room at the other end of the house. He jumped up, thinking it's sick the woman was, and followed her to the room to help her. He shut the door after him. As he was not coming back for a long time the son thought at last that he'd go and ask the father why he wasn't eating his supper. When he went into the room he saw no sign of his mother, saw nothing in the place but two legs from the knees down. He screamed out for his sister and she came.

"Oh, merciful God!" screamed the sister.

"Those are my father's legs! cried the brother, "and Mary, don't you know the stockings, sure you knitted them yourself, and don't I know the brogues very well?"

72

They called in the neighbours, and, to the terror of them all, they saw nothing but the two legs and feet of James Shea.

There was a wake over the remains that night, and the next day they buried the two legs. Some people advised the boy and girl never to sleep a night in the house, that their mother's soul was lost, and that was why she came and ate up the father, and she would eat themselves as well.

The two now started to walk the world, not caring much where they were going if only they escaped the mother. They stopped the first night at a farmer's house not far from Killarney. After supper a bed was made down for them by the fire, in the corner, and they lay there. About the middle of the night a great noise was heard outside, and the woman of the house called to her boys and servants to get up and go to the cow-house to know why the cows were striving to kill one another. Her own son rose first. When he and the two servant boys went out they saw the ghost of a woman, and she in chains. She made at them, and wasn't long killing the three.

Not seeing the boys come in, the farmer and his wife rose up, sprinkled holy water around the house, blessed themselves and went out, and there they saw the ghost in blue blazes and chains around her. In a coop outside by himself was a March cock. He flew down from his perch and crowed twelve times. That moment the ghost disappeared.

Now the neighbours were roused, and the news flew

around that the three boys were killed. The brother and sister didn't say a word to any one, but, rising up early, started on their journey, begging God's protection as they went. They never stopped nor stayed till they came to Rathmore, near Cork, and, going to a farmhouse, the boy asked for lodgings in God's name.

"I will give you lodgings in His name," said the farmer's wife.

She brought warm water for the two to wash their hands and feet, for they were tired and dusty. After supper a bed was put down for them, and about the same hour as the night before there was a great noise outside.

"Rise up and go out," said the farmer's wife; "some of the cows must be untied."

"I'll not go out at this hour of the night, if they are untied itself," said the man, "I'll stay where I am, if they kill one another, for it isn't safe to go out till the cock crows; after cock-crow I'll go out."

"That's true for you," said the farmer's wife, "and upon my word, before coming to bed, I forgot to sprinkle holy water in the room, and to bless myself."

So taking the bottle hanging near the bed, she sprinkled the water around the room and toward the threshold, and made the sign of the cross. The man didn't go out until cock-crow. The brother and sister went away early, and travelled all day. Coming evening they met a pleasant-looking man who stood before them in the road.

"You seem to be strangers," said he, "and where are you going?"

"We are strangers," said the boy, "and we don't know where to go."

"You need go no farther. I know you well, your home is in Iveragh. I am Saint Martin, sent from the Lord to protect you and your sister. You were going to draw the blood of a sheep in my honour, but your mother and brother made sport of you, and your mother wouldn't let you do what your father told you. You see what has come to them; they are lost for ever, both of them. Your father is saved in heaven, for he was a god man. Your mother will be here soon, and I'll put her in the way that she'll never trouble you again."

Taking a rod from his bosom and dipping it in a vial of holy water he drew a circle around the brother and sister. Soon they heard their mother coming, and then they saw her with chains on her, and the rattling was terrible, and flames were rising from her. She came to where they stood, and said: "Bad luck to you both, for being the cause of my misery."

"God forbid that," said Saint Martin. "It isn't they are the cause, but yourself, for you were always bad. You would not honour me, and now you must suffer for it."

He pulled out a book and began to read, and after he

read a few minutes he told her to depart and not be seen in Ireland again till the day of judgment. She rose in the air in flames of fire, and with such a noise that you'd think all the thunders of heaven were roaring and all the houses and walls in the kingdom were tumbling to the ground.

The brother and sister went on their knees and thanked Saint Martin. He blessed them and told them to rise, and taking a little table-cloth out of his bosom he said to the brother: "Take this cloth with you and keep it in secret. Let no one know that you have it. If you or your sister are in need go to your room, close the door behind you and bolt it. Spread out the cloth then, and plenty of everything to eat and drink will come to you. Keep the cloth with you always; it belongs to both of you. Now go home and live in the house that your father built, and let the priest come and celebrate Monday Mass in it, and live the life that your father lived before you."

The two came home, and brother and sister lived a good life. They married, and when either was in need that one had the cloth to fall back on, and their grand-children are living yet in Iveragh. And this is truth, every word of it, and it's often I heard my poor grand-mother tell this story, the Almighty God rest her soul, and she was the woman that wouldn't tell a lie. She knew James Shea and his wife very well.

John Cokeley and the Fairy

Jeremiah Curtin

There was a farmer in the parish of Firez whose name was John Cokeley. John was a great man for every kind of new information, and would go a long way of an evening to hear people read newspapers, but he didn't give in to stories or to what old people used to say.

Cokeley thought the house he had too small and wanted to put an addition to it. There was an old passage at one end of the house, and it's there he was going to build the addition. John had a gossip who used to go with the fairies, and this man passed the way when he was beginning the work.

"What's that you are doing?" asked the gossip.

"Don't you see what I am doing?" said Cokeley.

"Couldn't you put the addition to the other end of the house and leave this one alone?"

"That wouldn't suit me," answered John.

"You should leave the passage open so that every one could travel through it by day, and especially by night."

"That's foolish talk," said Cokeley.

"Very well," said the gossip, "you think so I suppose, but my word for it, you may be sorry in the end."

Cokeley finished the addition, and left a little hole in the wall near the fireplace, and it was there he kept his pipe and tobacco. One night on going to bed he put an ounce of tobacco in the hole (there was no one smoking in the house but himself). In the morning there was no bit of tobacco left, but in place of it the price, three-pence-ha'penny. He took great notice of that. A few weeks later he rose from his bed in the night and heard a great noise of horsemen outside. He opened the door and looked out, but if he did he saw nothing. He went to bed again, and wasn't long there when he began to be sore and feel very sick in himself. The gossip came to see him next day: "Well, John," said he, "you feel sick to-day."

"I do," said Cokeley.

"You had a right to stop in bed."

"How well you know of that," said Cokeley.

"I do; that much could not be done unknown to me.

When you turned back from the door last night there was a crowd between you and the bed as big as at any fair. They gave you only a warning this time, and you'll recover."

In a few weeks' time Cokeley was looking well again, but he got downhearted, took to drinking, and spent his means, so that at last he hadn't any cows on his land but what belonged to others. One May-day in the evening he was going to a neighbour's to collect grazing money that was due to him. When about three-quarters of the way—and the time was after sunset—a woman appeared opposite and took a great fall out of him. He was thrown on his face in the middle of the road and struck senseless. In half an hour he recovered, rose, and walked on; after going a short distance he was knocked a second time, and soon after he got the third fall. Cokeley didn't know for a full hour where he was; he hadn't his senses. When he came to himself he was in the middle of the road; he crawled to the side of it, then rose and went for his money. He didn't tell the man what had happened, made no delay, but hurried home and went to bed. He felt the strength parting from his body in the night, and was without any power to move next morning. His wife ran to doctors for cures, but no use for her. In a month's time all the neighbours said that Cokeley was fairy struck, and there was no cure. The wife went one day to Killarney, where she met the gossip.

"John is very bad again," said the gossip.

"He is," said she. "There is no one to do good for him if you don't."

"Oh, well," said the gossip, "I have a son of my own to assist, and he is nearer to me than what John is; I must look out for myself. John was struck very severely, and he may thank himself for it. He was not said by me, or he wouldn't have built in the passage, and wouldn't be where he is to-day. This is all the cure I can give you: Go home, get a tub of water, and bathe John nine nights with the one water, one night after another. When you have that done you'll not throw out the water till after midnight, when all are in bed. Take care that no one of your family is out of the house that night."

When John's wife was in the road coming home a man of the neighbours overtook her and they walked on together. There was a height within one mile of the house, from this they had a fine view of Cokeley's house and land— the time was after sunset—and to their surprise they saw John himself walking around in the garden as well and strong as ever, but when the wife came home she found him in bed sick and miserable.

"Were you out since morning, John?" asked she.

He only began to scold and look bitter at her. "How could a dead man leave the bed?" said he.

She prepared the tub of water in the corner of the house that day, and was bathing him for nine nights in the same water. She had a son fifteen or sixteen years of age who wasn't at home. He spent a night out very often, for he was working for people. She didn't think the boy would come that time, it was so late (about one o'clock in the morning). She began to throw out the water with a gallon.* There was a big flag outside the door; she threw the water on that. She had all out but the last gallon, when who should come but the son. When he stepped on the flag he was thrown heels over head and his leg broken. There was no doctor nearer than Killarney. When the mother went there next day she met the gossip.

"Well," said he, "you are worse now than ever. Didn't I tell you not to throw out that water when there was any one away from the house?"

"He slept out so often," said the mother, "that I was sure he wouldn't come that night."

"You may thank your friends and neighbours (of the other world) for being so strong, or your son's brains would be knocked out on that flag. He'll not be long recovering. The washing did no good to John, but he'll not leave you yet; he's very far back in the ranks. He will not go from you till he'll be the front man. Don't take too much care of him; he'll rob you."

When a neighbour came in the sick man had a tongue for any attorney, complaining of the wife, saying that she was

---

*A vessel for dipping water; it holds a few quarts.

only starving him. He would eat nothing from the poor woman but the best meat, butter and eggs; he should get a pint of whiskey every day. Every day he should be placed in a chair and brought to the fire between two persons. By looking at him you'd think there was nothing amiss with the man; besides, he had such an appetite and such a tongue for talking.

Soon the neighbours stopped coming, and didn't inquire. They used to see John Cokeley walking about the farm after sunset and before sunrise; they thought he was well again. This went on about four years, and the gossip who used to be with the fairies left this world altogether.

In the latter end the wife couldn't give the sick man what food he wanted, and he was raging; he kept the appetite all the time. She had a third cousin, a priest, and the priest came to see her.

"Oh, father, can't you do some good for my husband? Myself and my poor children are beggared from him."

"It isn't in my power to do good to that man," said the priest. "You must leave him there till he is taken from you."

She told how the husband abused her, what a tongue he had.

"Don't give him another tint of whiskey," said the priest, "nor meat, nor eggs. Give him what you and your children have."

The man gave a bitter look at the priest. The priest

gave a good morning and went home. After this the poor woman put no food before him but such as she and the children used. He was pining away and hadn't half the speech he had before, but he called her all the names he could think of. If he could have killed her he would.

It continued on in this way till one month before seven years were out, he pining, she breaking her heart with poverty.

This month he was sleeping all the time. They knew there was a change coming.

One midnight they heard a great crowd racing around the house, a noise of horses and people about the cross-road, and hurricanes of wind with terrible noises.

"Ah, I'll be going home soon," said he on the following morning, "I'm not sorry to leave you."

"Would you like to have a priest, John?" asked the wife.

"What would I do with a priest, woman?"

The uproar continued three nights. On the third evening he asked to eat— said he was starved. She gave him plenty of what she had and he ate it willingly, without any word at all from him. Herself and son and the little family, five altogether, were talking, and in an hour's time, when they didn't hear any sound from him, they went to the bed and found that it's dead he was, and they were not sorry after him; and sure why should they, for it wasn't John Cokeley that was in it at all.

The White Trout;
A Legend of Cong

Samuel Lover

There was wanst upon a time, long ago, a beautiful lady that lived in a castle upon the lake beyant, and they say she was promised to a king's son, and they wor to be married, when all of a sudden he was murthered, the crathur (Lord help us), and threwn into the lake above, and so, of course, he couldn't keep his promise to the fair lady —and more's the pity.

Well, the story goes that she went out iv her mind, bekase av loosin' the king's son —for she was tindher-hearted, God help her, like the rest iv us!—and pined away after him,

Abridged by Leslie Conron.

84

until at last, no one about seen her, good or bad; and the story wint that the fairies took her away.

Well, sir. in coorse o' time, the white throut, God bless it, was seen in the sthrame beyant, and sure the people didn't know what to think av the crathur, seein' as how a white throut was never heard av afor, nor since; and years upon years the throut was there, just where you seen it this blessed minit, longer nor I can tell—aye troth, and beyant the memory o' th' ouldest in the village.

At last the people began to think it must be a fairy; for what else could it be?— and no hurt nor harm was iver put an the white throut, until some wicked sinners of sojers kem to these parts, and laughed at all the people, and gibed and jeered them for thinkin' o' the likes; and one o' them in par-tic'lar (bad luck to him; God forgi' me for saying it!) swore he'd catch the throut and ate it for his dinner—the blackguard!

Well, what would you think o' the villainy of the sojer? Sure enough he cotch the throut, and away wid him home, and puts an the fryin'-pan, and into it he pitches the purty little thing. The throut squeeled all as one as a Christian crathur, and, my dear, you'd think the sojer id split his sides laughin'— for he was a harden'd villain; and when he thought one side was done, he turns it over to fry the other; and, what would you think, but the divil a taste of a burn was an it at all at all; and sure the sojer thought it was a *quare* throut that could not be briled. "But," says he, "I'll give it another turn by-and-by," little thinkin' what was in store for him, the haythen.

Well, when he thought that side was done he turns it agin, and lo and behould you, the divil a taste more done that side was nor the other. "Bad luck to me," says the sojer, "but that bates the world," says he; "but I'll thry you agin, my darlint," says he, "as cunnin' as you think yourself;" and so with that he turns it over and over, but not a sign of the fire was on the purty throut, "Well," says the desperate villain—(for sure, sir, only he was a desperate villain entirely, he might know he was doing a wrong thing, seein' that all his endeavours was no good)—"Well," says he, "my jolly little throut, maybe you're fried enough, though you don't seem over well dress'd; but you may be better than you look, like a singed cat, and a tit-bit afther all," says he; and with that he ups with his knife and fork to taste a piece o' the throut; but, my jew'l, the minit he puts his knife into the fish, there was a murtherin' screech, that you'd think the life id lave you if you hurd it, and away jumps the throut out av the fryin'-pan into the middle o' the flure; and an the spot where it fell, up riz a lovely lady—the beautifullest crathur that eyes ever seen, dressed in white, and a band o' goold in her hair, and a sthrame o' blood runnin' down her arm.

"Look where you cut me, you villain," says she, and she held out her arm to him—and, my dear, he thought the sight id lave his eyes.

"Couldn't you lave me cool and comfortable in the river where you snared me, and not disturb me in my duty?" says she.

Well, he thrimbled like a dog in a wet sack, and at last he stammered out somethin', and begged for his life, and ax'd her ladyship's pardin, and said he didn't know she was on duty, or he was too good a sojer not to know betther nor to meddle wid her.

"I *was* on duty, then," says the lady; "I was watchin' for my true love that is comin' by wather to me," says she, "an' if he comes while I'm away, an' that I miss iv him, I'll turn you into a pinkeen, and I'll hunt you up and down for evermore, while grass grows or wather runs."

Well the sojer thought the life id lave him, at the thoughts iv his bein' turned into a pinkeen, and begged for mercy; and with that says the lady—

"Renounce your evil coorses," says she, "you villain, or you'll repint it too late; be a good man for the futhur, and go to your duty* reg'lar, and now," says she, "take me back and put me into the river again, where you found me."

"Oh, my lady," says the sojer, "how could I have the

---

*The Irish peasant calls his attendance at the confessional "going to his duty."

heart to drownd a beautiful lady like you?"

But before he could say another word, the lady was vanished, and there he saw the little throut an the ground. Well he put it in a clean plate, and away he runs for the bare life, for fear her lover would come while she was away; and he run, and he run, even till he came to the cave agin, and threw the throut into the river. The minit he did, the wather was as red as blood for a little while, by rayson av the cut, I suppose, until the sthrame washed the stain away; and to this day there's a little red mark an the throut's side, where it was cut.*

Well, sir, from that day out the sojer was an altered man, and reformed his ways, and went to his duty reg'lar, and fasted three times a-week— though it was never fish he tuk an fastin' days, for afther the fright he got, fish id never rest an his stomach—savin' your presence.

But anyhow, he was an altered man, as I said before, and in coorse o' time he left the army, and turned hermit at last; and they say he used to pray evermore for the soul of the White Throut.

---

*The fish has really a red spot on its side.

The Legend
of Knockgrafton

T. Crofton Croker

There was once a poor man who
lived in the fertile glen of Aherlow, at the foot of the gloomy
Galtee mountains, and he had a great hump on his back: he
looked just as if his body had been rolled up and placed upon
his shoulders; and his head was pressed down with the weight
so much that his chin, when he was sitting, used to rest upon
his knees for support. The country people were rather shy of
meeting him in any lonesome place, for though, poor creature,
he was as harmless and as inoffensive as a new-born infant,

yet his deformity was so great that he scarcely appeared to be a human creature, and some ill-minded persons had set strange stories about him afloat. He was said to have a great knowledge of herbs and charms; but certain it was that he had a mighty skilful hand in plaiting straws and rushes into hats and baskets, which was the way he made his livelihood.

Lusmore—for that was the nickname put upon him by reason of his always wearing a sprig of fairy cap, or lusmore, in his little straw hat—would ever get a higher penny for his plaited-work than any one else, and perhaps that was the reason why some one, out of envy, had circulated the strange stories about him. Be that as it may, it happened that he was returning one evening from the pretty town of Cahir towards Cappagh; and as little Lusmore walked very slowly, on account of the great hump upon his back, it was quite dark when he came to the old moat of Knockgrafton, which stood on the right-hand side of his road. Tired and weary was he, and noways comfortable in his own mind at thinking how much farther he had to travel, and that he should be walking all the night; so he sat down under the moat to rest himself, and began looking mournfully enough upon the moon, which,

> "Rising in clouded majesty, at length
> Apparent Queen, unveil'd her peerless light,
> And o'er the dark her silver mantle threw."

Presently there rose a wild strain of unearthly melody upon the ear of little Lusmore. He listened, and he thought that he had never heard such ravishing music before. It was like the sound of many voices, each mingling and blending with the other so strangely that they seemed to be one, though all singing different strains, and the words of the song were these—

Da Luan, Da Mort, Da Luan, Da Mort, Da Luan, Da Mort;

when there would be a moment's pause, and then the round of melody went on again.

Lusmore listened attentively, scarcely drawing his breath lest he might lose the slightest note. He now plainly perceived that the singing was within the moat; and though at first it had charmed him so much, he began to get tired of hearing the same round sung over and over so often without any change. So availing himself of the pause when *Da Luan Da Mort*, had been sung three times, he took up the tune, and raised it with the words *augus Da Cadine*, and then went on singing with the voices inside of the moat, *Da Luan, Da Mort,* finishing the melody, when the pause again came, with *augus Da Cadine*.

The fairies within Knockgrafton—for the song was a fairy melody—when they heard this addition to the tune, were so much delighted that, with instant resolve, it was determined to bring the mortal among them, whose musical skill so far exceeded theirs, and little Lusmore was conveyed into their company with the eddying speed of a whirlwind.

Glorious to behold was the sight that burst upon him as he came down through the moat, twirling round and round and round with the lightness of a straw, to the sweetest music that kept time to his motion. The greatest honour was then paid him, for he was put up above all the musicians, and he had servants tending upon him, and everything to his heart's content, and a hearty welcome to all; and, in short, he was made as much of as if he had been the first man in the land.

Presently Lusmore saw a great consultation going forward among the fairies, and, notwithstanding all their civility, he felt very much frightened, until one, stepping out from the rest came up to him and said —

"Lusmore! Lusmore!
Doubt not, nor deplore,
For the hump which you bore
On your back is no more—!
Look down on the floor,
And view it, Lusmore!"

When these words were said, poor little Lusmore felt himself so light, and so happy, that he thought he could have bounded at one jump over the moon, like the cow in the history of the cat and the fiddle; and he saw, with inexpressible pleasure, his hump tumble down upon the ground from his shoulders. He then tried to lift up his head, and he did so with becoming caution, fearing that he might knock it against the ceiling of the grand hall, where he was. He looked round and round again with the greatest wonder and delight upon everything, which appeared more and more beautiful; and, overpowered at beholding such a resplendent scene, his head grew dizzy, and his eyesight became dim. At last he fell into a sound sleep, and when he awoke he found that it was broad daylight, the sun shining brightly, the birds singing sweetly; and that he was lying just at the foot of the moat of Knockgrafton, with the cows and sheep grazing peaceably round about him. The first thing Lusmore did, after saying his prayers, was to put his hand behind to feel for his hump, but no sign of one was there on his back, and he looked at himself with great pride, for he had now become a well-shaped, dapper little fellow, and more than that, found himself in a full suit of new clothes, which, he concluded, the fairies had made for him.

Towards Cappagh he went, stepping out as lightly, and springing up at every step, as if he had been all his life a dancing-master. Not a creature who met Lusmore knew him without his hump, and he had a great work to persuade every one that he was the same man—in truth he was not, so far as the outward appearance went.

Of course, it was not long before the story of Lusmore's hump got about, and a great wonder was made of it. Through the country, for miles round, it was the talk of every one, high and low.

One morning, as Lusmore was sitting contented enough at his cabin door, up came an old woman to him, and asked him if he could direct her to Cappagh.

"I need give you no directions, my good woman," said Lusmore, "for this is Cappagh; and whom may you want here?"

"I have come," said the woman, "out of Decie's country, in the county of Waterford, looking after one Lusmore, who, I have heard tell, had his hump taken off by the fairies; for there is a son of a gossip of mine who has got a hump on him that will be his death; and maybe, if he could use the same charm as Lusmore, the hump may be taken off him. And now I have told you the reason of my coming so far; 'tis to find out about this charm, if I can."

Lusmore, who was ever a good-natured little fellow, told the woman all the particulars, how he had raised the tune for the fairies at Knockgrafton, how his hump had been removed from his shoulders, and how he had got a new suit of clothes into the bargain.

The woman thanked him very much, and then went away quite happy and easy in her own mind. When she came back to her gossip's house, in the county of Waterford, she told her everything that Lusmore had said, and they put the little hump-backed man, who was a peevish and cunning creature from his birth, upon a car, and took him all the way across the country. It was a long journey, but they did not care for that, so the hump was taken from off him; and they brought him, just at nightfall, and left him under the old moat of Knockgrafton.

Jack Madden—for that was the humpy man's name—had not been sitting there long when he heard the tune going on within the moat much sweeter than before; for the fairies were singing in the way Lusmore had settled their music for them, and the song was going on: *Da Luan, Da Mort, Da Luan, Da Mort, Da Luan, Da Mort, augus Da Cadine*, without ever stopping. Jack Madden, who was in a great hurry to get rid of his hump, never thought of waiting until the fairies had done, or watching for a fit opportunity to raise the tune higher again than Lusmore had; so having heard them sing it over seven times without stopping, out he bawls, never minding the time or the humour of the tune, or how he could bring his words in properly, *augus Da Cadine, augus Da Hena*, thinking that if one day was good, two were better; and that if Lusmore had one new suit of clothes given him, he should have two.

No sooner had the words passed his lips than he was taken up and whisked into the moat with prodigious force; and the fairies came crowding round about him with great anger, screeching and screaming, and roaring out, "Who spoiled our tune? who spoiled our tune?" and one stepped up to him above all the rest, and said:

> "Jack Madden! Jack Madden!
> Your words came so bad in
> The tune we felt glad in; -
> This castle you're had in,
> That your life we may sadden;
> Here's two humps for Jack Madden!"

And twenty of the strongest fairies brought Lusmore's hump, and put it down upon poor Jack's back, over his own, where it became fixed as firmly as if it was nailed on with twelvepenny nails, by the best carpenter that ever drove one. Out of their castle they then kicked him; and in the morning, when Jack Madden's mother and her gossip came to look after their little man, they found him half dead, lying at the foot of the moat, with the other hump upon his back. Well to be sure, how they did look at each other; but they were afraid to say anything, lest a hump might be put upon their shoulders. Home they brought the unlucky Jack Madden with them, as downcast in their hearts and their looks as ever two gossips were; and what through the weight of his other hump, and the long journey, he died soon after, leaving, as they say, his heavy curse to any one who would go to listen to fairy tunes again.

The Brewery of Eggshells

T. Crofton Croker

It may be considered impertinent were I to explain what is meant by a changeling: both Shakespeare and Spenser have already done so and who is there unacquainted with the *Midsummer Night's Dream* and the *Fairy Queen*.

Now Mrs. Sullivan fancied that her youngest child had been exchanged by "fairies theft," to use Spenser's words, and certainly appearances warranted such a conclusion; for in one night her healthy, blue-eyed boy had become shrivelled up into almost nothing, and never ceased squalling and crying. This naturally made poor Mrs. Sullivan very unhappy; and all the neighbours, by way of comforting her, said that her own child was, beyond any kind of doubt, with the good people, and that one of themselves had been put in his place.

Mrs. Sullivan of course could not disbelieve what everyone told her, but she did not wish to hurt the thing; for although its face was so withered, and its body wasted away to a mere skeleton, it had still a strong resemblance to her own boy; she, therefore, could not find it in her heart to roast it alive on the griddle, or to burn its nose off with the red-hot tongs, or to throw it out in the snow on the road-side, notwith-standing these, and several like proceedings, were strongly recommended to her for the recovery of her child.

One day who should Mrs. Sullivan meet but a cunning woman, well known about the country by the name of Ellen Leah (or Grey Ellen). She had the gift, however she got it, of telling where the dead were, and what was good for the rest of their souls; and could charm away warts and wens, and do a great many wonderful things of the same nature.

"You're in grief this morning, Mrs. Sullivan," were the first words of Ellen Leah to her.

"You may say that, Ellen," said Mrs. Sullivan, "and good cause I have to be in grief, for there was my own fine child whipped off from me out of his cradle, without as much as 'by your leave' or 'ask your pardon,' and an ugly dony bit of a shrivelled-up fairy put in his place; no wonder, then, that you see me in grief, Ellen."

"Small blame to you, Mrs. Sullivan," said Ellen Leah, "but are you sure 'tis a fairy?"

"Sure!" echoed Mrs. Sullivan, "sure enough I am to my sorrow, and can I doubt my own two eyes? Every mother's soul must feel for me!"

"Will you take an old woman's advice?" said Ellen Leah, fixing her wild and mysterious gaze upon the unhappy mother; and, after a pause, she added: "But maybe you'll call it foolish?"

"Can you get me back my child—my own child, Ellen?" said Mrs. Sullivan with great energy.

"If you do as I bid you," returned Ellen Leah, "you'll know." Mrs. Sullivan was silent in expectation, and Ellen continued: "Put down the big pot, full of water, on the fire, and make it boil like mad; then get a dozen new-laid eggs, break them, and keep the shells, but throw away the rest. When that is done, put the shells in the pot of boiling water, and you will soon know whether it is your own boy or a fairy. If you find that it is a fairy in the cradle, take the red-hot poker and cram it down his ugly throat, and you will not have much trouble with him after that, I promise you."

Home went Mrs. Sullivan, and did as Ellen Leah desired. She put the pot on the fire, and plenty of turf under it, and set the water boiling at such a rate, that is ever water was red-hot, it surely was.

The child was lying, for a wonder, quite easy and quiet in the cradle, every now and then cocking his eye, that would twinkle as keen as a star in a frosty night, over at the great fire, and the big pot upon it; and he looked on with great attention at Mrs. Sullivan breaking the eggs and putting down the egg-shells to boil. At last he asked, with the voice of a very old man, "What are you doing, mammy?"

Mrs. Sullivan's heart, as she said herself, was up in her mouth ready to choke her, at hearing the child speak. But she contrived to put the poker in the fire, and to answer, without making any wonder at the words, "I'm brewing, a vick" (my son).

"And what are you brewing, mammy?" said the little imp, whose supernatural gift of speech now proved beyond question that he was a fairy substitute.

"I wish the poker was red," thought Mrs. Sullivan; but it was a large one, and took a long time heating; so she determined to keep him in talk until the poker was in a proper state to thrust down his throat, and therefore repeated the question.

"Is it what I'm brewing, a vick," said she, "you want to know?"

"Yes, mammy: what are you brewing?" returned the fairy.

"Egg-shells, a vick," said Mrs. Sullivan.

"Oh!" shrieked the imp, starting up in the cradle, and clapping his hands together, "I'm fifteen hundred years in the world, and I never saw a brewery of egg-shells before!" The poker was by this time quite red, and Mrs. Sullivan, seizing it, ran furiously towards the cradle; but somehow or other her foot slipped, and she fell flat on the floor, and the poker flew out of her hand to the other end of the house. However, she got up without much loss of time and went to the cradle, intending to pitch the wicked thing that was in it into the pot of boiling water, when there she saw her own child in a sweet sleep, one of his soft round arms rested upon the pillow—his features were as placid as if their repose had never been disturbed, save the rosy mouth, which moved with a gentle and regular breathing.

Who can tell the feelings of a mother when she looks upon her sleeping child? Why should I, therefore, endeavour to describe those of Mrs. Sullivan at again beholding her long-lost boy? The fountain of her heart overflowed with the excess of joy—and she wept!—tears trickled silently down her cheeks, nor did she strive to check them—they were tears not of sorrow, but of happiness.

Flory Cantillon's Funeral

T. Crofton Croker

The ancient burial-place of the Cantillon family was on an island in Ballyheigh Bay. This island was situated at no great distance from the shore, and at a remote period was overflowed in one of the encroachments which the Atlantic has made on that part of the coast of Kerry. The fishermen declare they have often seen the ruined walls of an old chapel beneath them in the water, as they sailed over the clear green sea, of a sunny afternoon. However this may be, it is well-known that the Cantillons were, like most other Irish families, strongly attached to their ancient burial-place; and this attachment led to the custom, when any of the family died, of carrying the corpse to the sea-side, where the coffin was left on the shore within reach of the tide. In the morning it had disappeared, being, as was traditionally believed, conveyed away by the ancestors of the deceased to their family tomb.

Connor Crowe, a county Clare man, was related to the Cantillons by marriage. "Connor Mac in Cruagh, of the seven quarters of Breintragh," as he was commonly called, and a proud man he was of the name. Connor, be it known, would drink a quart of salt water, for its medicinal virtues, before breakfast; and for the same reason, I suppose, double that quantity of raw whiskey between breakfast and night, which last he did with as little inconvenience to himself as any man in the barony of Moyferta; and were I to add Clanderalaw and Ibrickan, I don't think I should say wrong.

On the death of Florence Cantillon, Connor Crowe was determined to satisfy himself about the truth of this story of the old church under the sea: so when he heard the news of the old fellow's death, away with him to Ardfert, where Flory was laid out in high style, and a beautiful corpse he made.

Flory had been as jolly and as rollicking a boy in his day as ever was stretched, and his wake was in every respect worthy of him. There was all kind of entertainment, and all sort of diversion at it, and no less than three girls got husbands there—more luck to them. Everything was as it should be; all that side of the country, from Dingle to Tarbert, was at the funeral. The Keen was sung long and bitterly; and, according to the family custom, the coffin was carried to Ballyheigh strand, where it was laid upon the shore, with a prayer for the repose of the dead.

The mourners departed, one group after another, and at last Connor Crowe was left alone: he then pulled out his whiskey bottle, his drop of comfort, as he called it, which he required, being in grief; and down he sat upon a big stone that was sheltered by a projecting rock, and partly concealed from view, to await with patience the appearance of the ghostly undertakers.

The evening came on mild and beautiful. He whistled an old air which he had heard in his childhood, hoping to keep idle fears out of his head; but the wild strain of that melody brought a thousand recollections with it, which only made the twilight appear more pensive.

"If 'twas near the gloomy tower of Dunmore, in my own sweet country, I was," said Connor Crowe, with a sigh, "one might well believe that the prisoners, who were murdered long ago there in the vaults under the castle, would be the hands to carry off the coffin out of envy, for never a one of them was buried decently, nor had as much as a coffin amongst them all. 'Tis often, sure enough, I have heard lamentations and great mourning coming from the vaults of Dunmore Castle; but," continued he, after fondly pressing his lips to the mouth of his companion and silent comforter, the whiskey bottle, "didn't I know all the time well enough, 'twas the dismal sounding waves working through the cliffs and hollows of the rocks, and fretting themselves to foam. Oh, then, Dunmore Castle, it is you that are the gloomy-looking tower on a gloomy day, with the gloomy hills behind you; when one has gloomy thoughts on their heart, and sees you like a ghost rising out of the smoke made by the kelp burners on the strand, there is, the Lord save us! as fearful a look about you as about the Blue Man's Lake at midnight. Well, then, anyhow," said Connor, after a pause, "is it not a blessed night, though surely the moon looks mighty pale in the face? St. Senan himself between us and all kinds of harm."

It was, in truth, a lovely moonlight night; nothing was to be seen around but the dark rocks, and the white pebbly beach, upon which the sea broke with a hoarse and melancholy murmur. Connor, notwithstanding his frequent draughts, felt rather queerish, and almost began to repent his curiosity. It was certainly a solemn sight to behold the black coffin resting upon the white strand. His imagination gradually converted the deep moaning of old ocean into a mournful wail for the dead, and from the shadowy recesses of the rocks he imaged forth strange and visionary forms.

As the night advanced, Connor became weary with watching. He caught himself more than once in the act of nodding, when suddenly giving his head a shake, he would look towards the black coffin. But the narrow house of death remained unmoved before him.

It was long past midnight, and the moon was sinking into the sea, when he heard the sound of many voices, which gradually became stronger, above the heavy and monotonous roll of the sea. He listened, and presently could distinguish a Keen of exquisite sweetness, the notes of which rose and fell with the heaving of the waves, whose deep murmur mingled with and supported the strain!

The Keen grew louder and louder, and seemed to approach the beach, and then fell into a low, plaintive wail. As it ended Connor beheld a number of strange and, in the dim light, mysterious-looking figures emerge from the sea, and surround the coffin, which they prepared to launch into the water. "This comes of marrying with the creatures of earth,' said one of the figures, in a clear, yet hollow tone.

"True," replied another, with a voice still more fearful, "our king would never have commanded his gnawing white-toothed waves to devour the rocky roots of the island ceme-tery, had not his daughter, Durfulla, been buried there by her mortal husband!"

"But the time will come," said a third, bending over the coffin,

When mortal eye—our work shall spy,
And mortal ear—our dirge shall hear."

"Then," said a fourth, "our burial of the Cantillons is at an end for ever!"

As this was spoken the coffin was borne from the beach by a retiring wave, and the company of sea people prepared to follow it; but at the moment one chanced to discover Connor Crowe, as fixed with wonder and as motionless with fear as the stone on which he sat.

"The time is come," cried the unearthly being, "the time is come; a human eye looks on the forms of ocean, a human ear has heard their voice. Farewell to the Cantillons; the sons of the sea are no longer doomed to bury the dust of the earth!"

One after the other turned slowly round, and regarded Connor Crowe, who still remained as if bound by a spell. Again arose their funeral song; and on the next wave they followed the coffin. The sound of the lamentation died away, and at length nothing was heard but the rush of waters. The coffin and the train of sea people sank over the old churchyard, and never, since the funeral of old Flory Cantillon, have any of the family been carried to the strand of Ballyheigh, for conveyance to their rightful burial-place, beneath the waves of the Atlantic.

The Lepracaun;
or Fairy Shoemaker
William Allingham

I.
Little Cowboy, what have you heard,
     Up on the lonely rath's green mound?
Only the plaintive yellow bird*
     Sighing in sultry fields around,
Chary, chary, chary, chee-ee! —
Only the grasshopper and the bee? —

     "Tip, tap, rip-rap,
     Tick-a-tack-too!
Scarlet leather, sewn together,
     This will make a shoe.

"Yellow bird," the yellow-bunting, or yorlin.

Left, right, pull it tight;
  Summer days are warm;
Underground in winter,
  Laughing at the storm!"
Lay your ear close to the hill.
Do you not catch the tiny clamour,
Busy click of an elfin hammer,
Voice of the Lepracaun singing shrill
  As he merrily plies his trade?
   He's a span
   And a quarter in height.
Get him in sight, hold him tight,
   And you're a made
    Man!

II.
You watch your cattle the summer day,
Sup on potatoes, sleep in the hay;
  How would you like to roll in your car-
riage,
  Look for a duchess's daughter in mar-
riage?
Seize the Shoemaker—then you may!

"Big boots a-hunting,
  Sandals in the hall,
White for a wedding-feast,
  Pink for a ball.
This way, that way,
  So we make a shoe;
Getting rich every stitch,
  Tick-tack-too!"
Nine-and-ninety treasure-crocks
This keen miser-fairy hath,
Hid in mountains, woods, and rocks,
Ruin and round-tow'r, cave and rath,
  And where the cormorants build;
    From times of old
    Guarded by him;
    Each of them fill'd
    Full to the brim
      With gold!

III.
I caught him at work one day, myself,
  In the castle-ditch, where foxglove grows—
A wrinkled, wizen'd, and bearded Elf,
  Spectacles stuck on his pointed nose,
  Silver buckles to his hose,

Leather apron— shoe in his lap—
      "Rip-rap, tip-tap,
       Tick-tack-too!
     (A grasshopper on my cap!
        Away the moth flew!)
     Buskins for a fairy prince,
         Brogues for his son—
     Pay me well, pay me well,
        When the job is done!"
The rogue was mine, beyond a doubt.
I stared at him; he stared at me;
"Servant, Sir!" "Humph!" says he,
        And pull'd a snuff-box out.
He took a long pinch, look's better pleased,
       The queer little Lepracaun;
Offer'd the box with a whimsical grace,—
Pouf! he flung the dust in my face,
        And, while I sneezed,
           Was gone!

Master and Man

T. Crofton Croker

Billy Mac Daniel was once as likely a young man as ever shook his brogue at a patron,* emptied a quart, or handled a shillelagh; fearing for nothing but the want of drink; caring for nothing but who should pay for it; and thinking of nothing but how to make fun over it; drunk or sober, a word and a blow was ever the way with Billy Mac Daniel; and a mighty easy way it is of either getting into or of ending a dispute. More is the pity that, through the means of his thinking, and fearing, and caring for nothing, this same Billy Mac Daniel fell into bad company; for surely the

---

*A festival held in honour of some patron saint.

good people are the worst of all company of any one could come across.

It so happened that Billy was going home one clear frosty night not long after Christmas; the moon was round and bright; and although it was as fine a night as he could wish for, he felt pinched with cold. "By my word," chattered Billy, "a drop of good liquor would be no bad thing to keep a man's soul from freezing in him; and I wish I had a full measure of the best."

"Never wish it twice, Billy," said a little man in a three-cornered hat, bound all about with gold lace, and with great silver buckles in his shoes, so big that it was a wonder how he could carry them, and he held out a glass as big as himself, filled with as good liquor as ever eye looked on or lip tasted.

"Success, my little fellow," said Billy Mac Daniel, nothing daunted, though well he knew the little man to belong to the good people; "here's your health, any way, and thank you kindly; no matter who pays for the drink;" and he took the glass and drained it to the very bottom without ever taking a second breath to it.

"Success," said the little man; "and you're heartily welcome, Billy; but don't think to cheat me as you have done others—out with your purse and pay me like a gentleman."

"Is it I pay you?" said Billy; "could I not just take you up and put you in my pocket as easily as a blackberry?"

"Billy Mac Daniel," said the little man getting very angry, "you shall be my servant for seven years and a day, and that is the way I will be paid; so make ready to follow me."

When Billy heard this he began to be very sorry for having used such bold words towards the little man; and he felt himself, yet could not tell how, obliged to follow the little man the live-long night about the country, up and down, and over hedge and ditch, and through bog and brake, without any rest.

When morning began to dawn the little man turned round to him and said, "You may now go home, Billy, but on your peril don't fail to meet me in the Fort-field to-night; or if you do it may be the worse for you in the long run. If I find you a good servant, you will find me an indulgent master."

Home went Billy Mac Daniel; and though he was tired and weary enough, never a wink of sleep could he get for thinking of the little man; but he was afraid not to do his bidding, so up he got in the evening, and away he went to the Fort-field. He was not long there before the little man came towards him and said, "Billy, I want to go a long journey to-night; so saddle one of my horses, and you may saddle another for yourself, as you are to go along with me, and may be tired after your walk last night."

Billy thought this very considerate of his master, and thanked him accordingly; "But," said he, "if I may be so bold, sir, I would ask which is the way to your stable, for never a thing do I see but the fort here, and the old thorn tree in the corner of the field, and the stream running at the bottom of the hill, with the bit of bog over against us."

"Ask no questions, Billy," said the little man, "but go over to that bit of bog, and bring me two of the strongest rushes you can find."

Billy did accordingly, wondering what the little man would be at; and he picked two of the stoutest rushes he could find, with a little bunch of brown blossom stuck at the side of each, and brought them back to his master.

"Get up, Billy," said the little man, taking one of the rushes from him and striding across it.

"Where shall I get up, please your honour?" said Billy.

"Why, upon horseback, like me, to be sure," said the little man.

"Is it after making a fool of me you'd be," said Billy, "bidding me to get a horseback upon that bit of rush? May be you want to persuade me that the rush I pulled but a while ago out of the bog over there is a horse?"

"Up! up! and no words," said the little man, looking very angry; "the best horse you ever rode was but a fool to it." So Billy, thinking all this was a joke, and fearing to vex his master, straddled across the rush. "Borram! Borram! Borram!" cried the little man three times (which, in English, means to become great), and Billy did the same after him; presently the rushes swelled up into fine horses, and away they went full speed; but Billy, who had put the rush between his legs, without much minding how he did it, found himself sitting on horseback the wrong way, which was rather awkward, with his face to the horse's tail; and so quickly had his steed started off with him that he had no power to turn round, and there was therefore nothing for it but to hold on by the tail.

At last they came to their journey's end, and stopped at the gate of a fine house. "Now, Billy," said the little man, "do as you see me do, and follow me close; but as you did not know your horse's head from his tail, mind that your own head does not spin round until you can't tell whether you are standing on it or on your heels: for remember that old liquor, though able to make a cat speak, can make a man dumb."

The little man then said some queer kind of words, out of which Billy could make no meaning; but he contrived to say them after him for all that; and in they both went through the key-hole of the door, and through one key-hole after another, until they got into the wine-cellar, which was well stored with all kinds of wine.

The little man fell to drinking as hard as he could, and Billy, noway disliking the example, did the same. "The best of all masters are you, surely," said Billy to him; "no matter who is the next; and well pleased will I be with your service if you continue to give me plenty to drink."

"I have made no bargain with you," said the little man, "and will make none; but up and follow me." Away they went, through key-hole after key-hole; and each mounting upon the rush which he had left at the hall door, scampered off, kicking the clouds before them like snow-balls, as soon as the words, "Borram, Borram, Borram," had passed their lips.

When they came back to the Fort-field the little man dismissed Billy, bidding him to be there the next night at the same hour. Thus did they go on, night after night, shaping their course one night here, and another night there; some-times north, and sometimes east, and sometimes south, until there was not a gentleman's wine-cellar in all Ireland they had not visited, and could tell the flavour of every wine in it as well—ay, better than the butler himself.

One night when Billy Mac Daniel met the little man as usual in the Fort-field, and was going to the bog to fetch the horses for their journey, his master said to him, "Billy, I shall want another horse to-night, for may be we may bring back more company than we take." So Billy, who now knew better than to question any order given to him by his master, brought a third rush, much wondering who it might be that would trav-el back in their company, and whether he was about to have a fellow-servant. "If I have," thought Billy, "he shall go and fetch the horses from the bog every night; for I don't see why I am not, every inch of me, as good a gentleman as my master."

Well, away they went, Billy leading the third horse, and never stopped until they came to a snug farmer's house, in the county Limerick, close under the old castle of Carrigogunniel, that was built, they say, by the great Brian Boru. Within the house there was great carousing going forward, and the little man stopped outside for some time to listen; then turning round all of a sudden, said, "Billy, I will be a thousand years old to-morrow!"

"God bless us, sir," said Billy; "will you?"

"Don't say these words again, Billy," said the little old man, "or you will be my ruin for ever. Now Billy, as I will be a thousand years in the world to-morrow, I think it is full time for me to get married."

"I think so too, without any kind of doubt at all," said Billy, "if ever you mean to marry."

"And to that purpose," said the little man, "have I come all the way to Carrigogunniel; for in this house, this very night, is young Darby Riley going to be married to Bridget Rooney; and as she is a tall and comely girl, and has come of decent people, I think of marrying her myself, and taking her off with me."

"And what will Darby Riley say to that?" said Billy.

"Silence!" said the little man, putting on a mighty severe look; "I did not bring you here with me to ask questions;" and without holding further argument, he began saying the queer words which had the power of passing him through the key-hole as free as air, and which Billy thought himself mighty clever to be able to say after him.

In they both went; and for the better viewing the company, the little man perched himself up as nimbly as a cocksparrow upon one of the big beams which went across the house over all their heads, and Billy did the same upon another facing him; but not being much accustomed to roosting in such a place, his legs hung down as untidy as may be, and it was quite clear he had not taken pattern after the way in which the little man had bundled himself up together. If the little man had been a tailor all his life he could not have sat more contentedly upon his haunches.

There they were, both master and man, looking down upon the fun that was going forward; and under them were the priest and piper, and the father of Darby Riley, with Darby's two brothers and his uncle's son; and there were both the father and the mother of Bridget Rooney, and proud enough the old couple were that night of their daughter, as good right they had; and her four sisters, with brand new ribbons in their caps, and her three brothers all looking as clean and as clever as any three boys in Munster—and there were uncles and aunts, and gossips and cousins enough besides to make a full house of it—and plenty was there to eat and drink on the table for every one of them, if they had been double the number.

Now it happened, just as Mrs. Rooney had helped his reverence to the first cut of the pig's head which was placed before her, beautifully bolstered up with white savoys, that the bride gave a sneeze, which made every one at the table start, but not a soul said "God bless us." All thinking that the priest would have done so, as he ought if he had done his duty, no one wished to take the word out of his mouth, which, unfortunately, was preoccupied with pig's head and greens. And after a moment's pause the fun and merriment of the bridal feast went on without the pious benediction.

Of this circumstance both Billy and his master were no inattentive spectators from their exalted stations. "Ha!" exclaimed the little man, throwing one leg from under him with a joyous flourish, and his eye twinkled with a strange light, whilst his eyebrows became elevated into the curvature of Gothic arches; "Ha!" said he, leering down at the bride, and then up at Billy, "I have half of her now, surely. Let her sneeze but twice more, and she is mine, in spite of priest, mass-book, and Darby Riley."

Again the fair Bridget sneezed; but it was so gently, and she blushed so much, that few except the little man took, or seemed to take, any notice; and no one thought of saying "God bless us."

Billy all this time regarded the poor girl with a most

rueful expression of countenance; for he could not help thinking what a terrible thing it was for a nice young girl of nineteen, with large blue eyes, transparent skin, and dimpled cheeks, suffused with health and joy, to be obliged to marry an ugly little bit of a man, who was a thousand years old, barring a day.

At this critical moment the bride gave a third sneeze, and Billy roared out with all his might, "God save us!" Whether this exclamation resulted from his soliloquy, or from the mere force of habit, he never could tell exactly himself; but no sooner was it uttered than the little man, his face glowing with rage and disappointment, sprung from the beam on which he had perched himself, and shrieking out in the shrill voice of a cracked bagpipe, "I discharge you from my service, Billy Mac Daniel—take that for your wages," gave poor Billy a most furious kick in the back, which sent his unfortunate servant sprawling upon his face and hands right in the middle of the supper table.

If Billy was astonished, how much more so was every one of the company into which he was thrown with so little ceremony. But when they heard his story, Father Cooney laid down his knife and fork, and married the young couple out of hand with all speed; and Billy Mac Daniel danced the Rinka at their wedding, and plenty did he drink at it too, which was what he thought more of than dancing.

Far Darrig in Donegal

Letitia Maclintock

Pat Diver, the tinker, was a man well-accustomed to a wandering life, and to strange shelters; he had shared the beggar's blanket in smoky cabins; he had crouched beside the still in many a nook and corner where poteen was made on the wild Innishowen mountains; he had even slept on the bare heather, or on the ditch, with no roof over him but the vault of heaven; yet were all his nights of adventure tame and commonplace when compared with one especial night.

During the day preceding that night, he had mended all the kettles and saucepans in Moville and Greencastle, and was on his way to Culdaff, when night overtook him on a lonely mountain road.

He knocked at one door after another asking for a night's lodging, while he jingled the halfpence in his pocket, but was everywhere refused.

Where was the boasted hospitality of Innishowen, which he had never known to fail? It was of no use to be able to pay when the people seemed so churlish. Thus thinking, he made his way towards a light a little further on, and knocked at another cabin door.

An old man and woman were seated one at each side of the fire. "Will you be pleased to give me a night's lodging, sir?" asked Pat respectfully.

"Can you tell a story?" returned the old man.

"No, then, sir, I canna say I'm good at story-telling," replied the puzzled tinker.

"Then you maun just gang further, for none but them that can tell a story will get in here."

This reply was made in so decided a tone that Pat did not attempt to repeat his appeal, but turned away reluctantly to resume his weary journey.

"A story, indeed," muttered he. "Auld wives fables to please the weans!"

As he took up his bundle of tinkering implements, he observed a barn standing rather behind the dwelling-house, and, aided by the rising moon, he made his way towards it.

It was a clean, roomy barn, with a piled-up heap of straw in one corner. Here was a shelter not to be despised; so Pat crept under the straw, and was soon asleep.

He could not have slept very long when he was awakened by the tramp of feet, and, peeping cautiously through a crevice in his straw covering, he saw four immensely tall men enter the barn, dragging a body, which they threw roughly upon the floor.

They next lighted a fire in the middle of the barn, and fastened the corpse by the feet with a great rope to a beam in the roof. One of them then began to turn it slowly before the fire. "Come on," said he, addressing a gigantic fellow, the tallest of the four—"I'm tired; you be to tak' your turn."

"Faix an' troth, I'll no turn him," replied the big man. "There's Pat Diver in under the straw, why wouldn't he tak' his turn?"

With hideous clamour the four men called the wretched Pat, who, seeing there was no escape, thought it was his wisest plan to come forth as he was bidden.

"Now, Pat," said they, "you'll turn the corpse, but if you let him burn you'll be tied up there and roasted in his place."

Pat's hair stood on end, and the cold perspiration poured from his forehead, but there was nothing for it but to perform his dreadful task.

Seeing him fairly embarked in it, the tall men went away. Soon, however, the flames rose so high as to singe the rope, and the corpse fell with a great thud upon the fire, scattering the ashes and embers, and extracting a howl of anguish from the miserable coo, who rushed to the door, and ran for his life.

He ran on until he was ready to drop with fatigue, when, seeing a drain overgrown with tall, rank grass, he thought he would creep in there and lie hidden till morning.

But he was not many minutes in the drain before he heard the heavy tramping again, and the four men came up with their burthen, which they laid down on the edge of the drain.

"I'm tired," said one, to the giant; "it's your turn to carry him a piece now."

"Faix and troth, I'll no carry him," replied he, "but there's Pat Diver in the drain, why wouldn't he come out and tak' his turn?"

"Come out, Pat, come out," roared all the men, and Pat, almost dead with fright, crept out.

He staggered on under the weight of the corpse until he reached Kiltown Abbey, a ruin festooned with ivy, where the brown owl hooted all night long, and the forgotten dead slept around the walls under dense, matted tangles of brambles and ben-weed.

No one ever buried there now, but Pat's tall companions turned into the wild graveyard, and began digging a grave.

Pat, seeing them thus engaged, thought he might once more try to escape, and climbed up into a hawthorn tree in the fence, hoping to be hidden in the boughs.

"I'm tired," said the man who was digging the grave; "here, take the spade," addressing the big man, "it's your turn."

"Faix an' troth, it's no my turn," replied he, as before. "There's Pat Diver in the tree, why wouldn't he come down and tak' his turn?"

Pat came down to take the spade, but just then the cocks in the little farmyards and cabins round the abbey began to crow, and the men looked at one another.

"We must go," said they, "and well is it for you, Pat Diver, that the cocks crowed, for if they had not, you'd just ha' been bundled into that grave with the corpse."

Two months passed, and Pat had wandered far and wide over the county Donegal, when he chanced to arrive at Raphoe during a fair.

Among the crowd that filled the Diamond he came suddenly on the big man.

"How are you, Pat Diver?" said he, bending down to look into the tinker's face.

"You've the advantage of me, sir, for I havna' the pleasure of knowing you," faltered Pat.

"Do you not know me, Pat?" Whisper—"When you go back to Innishowen, you'll have a story to tell!"

Daniel O'Rourke

T. Crofton Croker

People may have heard of the renowned adventures of Daniel O'Rourke, but how few are there who know that the cause of all his perils, above and below, was neither more nor less than his having slept under the walls of the Pooka's tower. I knew the man well. He lived at the bottom of Hungry Hill, just at the right-hand side of the road as you go towards Bantry. An old man was he, at the time he told me the story, with grey hair and a red nose; and it was on the 25th of June 1813 that I heard it from his own lips, as he sat smoking his pipe under the old poplar tree, on as fine an evening as ever shone from the sky. I was going to visit the caves in Dursey Island, having spent the morning at Glengariff.

"I am often *axed* to tell it, sir," said he, "so that this is not the first time. The master's son, you see, had come from beyond foreign parts in France and Spain, as young gentlemen used to go before Buonaparte or any such was heard of; and sure enough there was a dinner given to all the people on the ground, gentle and simple, high and low, rich and poor. The *ould* gentlemen were the gentlemen after all, saving your honour's presence. They'd swear at a body a little, to be sure, and, may be, give one a cut of a whip now and then, but we were no losers by it in the end;—and they were so easy and civil, and kept such rattling houses, and thousands of welcomes;—and there was no grinding for rent, and there was hardly a tenant on the estate that did not taste of his landlord's bounty often and often in a year; but now it's another thing. No matter for that, sir, for I'd better be telling you my story.

"Well, we had everything of the best, and plenty of it; and we ate, and we drank, and we danced, and the young master by the same token danced with Peggy Barry, from the Bohereen—a lovely young couple they were, though they are both low enough now. To make a long story short, I got, as a body may say, the same thing as tipsy almost, for I can't remember ever at all, no ways, how it was I left the place; only I did leave it, that's certain. Well, I thought, for all that, in myself, I'd just step to Molly Cronohan's, the fairy woman, to

Grass-covered fairy fort, Enfield. Photographer: Ivan O'Driscoll. Lonely places, where the good people enter and exit the fairy world, can still be found in the Irish countryside.

Top: The burren, near Kinvara. Photographer: Peter Zoeller.

Right: Glencolumbkille, Co. Donegal. Photographer: Christopher Hill.

Cliffs of Moher, Co. Clare. Photographer: Christopher Hill.

Inishbofin Island, Co. Galway. Photographer: Jamie Blandford.

Mist Over Ladies View, Killarney. Photographer: Peter Blake.

Grazing white horse in a rainbow-covered field. Photographer: Peter Zoeller.

speak a word about the bracket heifer that was bewitched; and so as I was crossing the stepping-stones of the ford of Ballyashenogh, and was looking up at the stars and blessing myself—for why? it was Lady-day—I missed my foot, and souse I fell into the water. 'Death alive!' thought I, 'I'll be drowned now!' However, I began swimming, swimming, swimming away for the dear life, till at last I got ashore, some-how or other, but never the one of me can tell how, upon a *dissolute* island.

"I wandered and wandered about there, without know-ing where I wandered, until at last I got into a big bog. The moon was shining as bright as day, or your fair lady's eyes, sir (with your pardon for mentioning her), and I looked east and west, and north and south, and every way, and nothing did I see but bog, bog, bog—I could never find out how I got into it; and my heart grew cold with fear, for sure and certain I was that it would be my *berrin* place. So I sat down upon a stone which, as good luck would have it, was close by me, and I began to scratch my head, and sing the *Ullagone*—when all of a sudden the moon grew black, and I looked up, and saw something for all the world as if it was moving down between me and it, and I could not tell what it was. Down it came with a pounce, and looked at me full in the face; and what was it but an eagle? as fine a one as ever flew from the kingdom of Kerry. So he looked at me in the face, and says he to me,

'Daniel O'Rourke,' says he, 'how do you do? 'Very well, I thank you, sir,' says I; ' I hope you're well;' wondering out of my senses all the time how an eagle came to speak like a Christian. 'What brings you here, Dan,' says he. 'Nothing at all, sir,' says I; 'only I wish I was safe home again.' 'Is it out of the island you want to go, Dan?' says he. ''Tis, sir,' says I: so I up and told him how I had taken a drop too much, and fell into the water; how I swam to the island; and how I got into the bog and did not know my way out of it. 'Dan,' says he, after a minute's thought, 'though it is very improper for you to get drunk on Lady-day, yet as you are a decent sober man, who 'tends mass well, and never flings stones at me or mine, nor cries out after us in the fields—my life for yours,' says he; 'so get up on my back, and grip me well for fear you'd fall off, and I'll fly you out of the bog.' 'I am afraid.' says I, 'your honour's making game of me; for who ever heard of riding horseback on an eagle before?' 'Pon the honour of a gentleman,' says he, putting his right foot on his breast, 'I am quite in earnest: and so now either take my offer or starve in the bog—beside, I see that your weight is sinking the stone.'

"It was true enough as he said, for I found the stone every minute going from under me. I had no choice; so thinks I to myself, faint heart never won fair lady, and this is fair per-suadance. 'I thank your honour,' says I, 'for the loan of your civility; and I'll take your kind offer.' I therefore mounted upon the back of the eagle, and held him tight enough by the throat, and up he flew in the air like a lark. Little I knew the trick he was going to serve me. Up—up—up, God knows how far up he flew. 'Why then,' said I to him—thinking he did not know the right road home—very civilly, because why? I was in his power entirely; 'sir,' says I, 'please your honour's glory, and with humble submission to your better judgment, if you'd fly down a bit, you're now just over my cabin, and I could be put down there, and many thanks to your worship.'

" '*Arrah*, Dan,' said he, 'do you think me a fool? Look down in the next field, and don't you see two men and a gun? By my word it would be no joke to be shot this way, to oblige a drunken blackguard that I picked up off of a could stone in a bog.' "Bother you' said I to myself, but I did not speak out, for where was the use? Well, sir, up he kept, flying, flying, and I asking him every minute to fly down, and all to no use. 'Where in the world are you going, sir?' says I to him. 'Hold your tongue, Dan,' says he: 'mind your own business, and don't be interfering with the business of other people.' 'Faith, this is my business, I think,' says I. 'Be quiet, Dan,' says he: so I said no more.

"At last where should we come to, but to the moon itself. Now you can't see it from this, but there is, or there was in my time, a reaping-hook sticking out of the side of the moon, this way (drawing the figure thus O¬ on the ground with the end of his stick).

" 'Dan,' said the eagle, 'I'm tired with this long fly; I had no notion 'twas so far.' 'And my lord, sir,' said I, 'who in the world axed you to fly so far—was it I? did not I beg and pray and beseech you to stop half an hour ago?' 'There's no use talking, Dan.' said he; 'I'm tired bad enough, so you must get off, and sit down on the moon until I rest myself.' 'Is it sit down on the moon?' said I; 'is it upon that little round thing, then? why, then, syre I'd fall off in a minute, and be kilt, and split, and smashed all to bits; you are a vile deceiver—so you are.' 'Not at all, Dan,' said he; 'you can catch fast hold of the reaping-hook that's sticking out of the side of the moon, and 'twill keep you up.' 'I won't then,' said I. 'May be not,' said he, quite quiet. 'If you don't, my man, I shall just give you a shake, and one slap of my wing, and send you down to the ground, where every bone in your body will be smashed as small as a drop of dew on a cabbage-leaf in the morning.' 'Why, then, I'm in a fine way,' said I to myself, 'ever to have come along with the likes of you;' and so giving him a hearty curse in Irish, for fear he'd know what I said, I got off his back with a heavy heart, took hold of the reaping-hook, and sat down upon the moon, and a mighty cold seat it was, I can tell you that.

"When he had me there fairly landed, he turned about on me, and said, 'Good morning to you, Daniel O'Rourke,' said he; 'I think I've nicked you fairly now. You robbed my nest last year' ('twas true enough for him, but how he found it out is hard to say), 'and in return you are freely welcome to cool your heels dangling upon the moon like a cockthrow.'

" 'Is that all, and is this the way you leave me, you brute, you,' says I. 'You ugly unnatural baste, and is this the way you serve me at last? Bad luck to yourself, with your hook'd nose, and to all your breed, you blackguard.' 'Twas all to no manner of use; he spread out his great big wings, burst out a laughing, and flew away like lightning. I bawled after him to stop; but I might have called and bawled for ever, without his minding me. Away he went, and I never saw him from that day to this—sorrow fly away with him! You may be sure I was in a disconsolate condition, and kept roaring out for the bare grief, when all at once a door opened right in the middle of the moon, creaking on its hinges as if it had not been opened for a month before, I suppose they never thought of greasing 'em, and out there walks—who do you think, but the man in the moon himself? I knew him by his bush.

" 'Good morrow to you, Daniel O'Rourke,' said he; 'how do you do?' 'Very well, thank your honour,' said I. 'I hope your honour's well.' 'What brought you here, Dan?' said he. So I told him how I was overtaken in liquor at the master's, and how I was cast on a dissolute island, and how I lost my way in the bog, and how the thief of an eagle promised to fly me out of it, and how, instead of that, he had fled me up to the moon.

" 'Dan,' said the man in the moon, taking a pinch of

snuff when I was done, 'you must not stay here.' 'Indeed, sir,' says I, ''tis much against my will I'm here at all; but how am I to go back?' 'That's your business,' said he; 'Dan, mine is to tell you that here you must not stay; so be off in less than no time.' 'I'm doing no harm,' says I, 'only holding on hard by the reaping-hook, lest I fall off.' 'That's what you must not do, Dan,' says he. 'Pray, sir,' says I, 'may I ask how many you are in family, that you would not give a poor traveller lodging: I'm sure 'tis not so often you're troubled with strangers coming to see you, for 'tis a long way.' 'I'm by myself, Dan,' says he; 'but you'd better let go the reaping-hook.' 'Faith, and with your leave,' says I, 'I'll not let go the grip, and the more you bids me, the more I won't let go;—so I will.' 'You had better, Dan,' says he again. 'Why, then, my little fellow,' says I, taking the whole weight of him with my eye from head to foot, 'there are two words to that bargain; and I'll not budge, but you may if you like.' 'We'll see how that is to be,' says he; and back he went giving the door such a great bang after him (for it was plain he was huffed) that I thought the moon and all would fall down with it.

"Well, I was preparing myself to try strength with him, when back again he comes, with the kitchen cleaver in his hand, and, without saying a word, he gives two bangs to the handle of the reaping-hook that was keeping me up, and *whap*! it came in two. 'Good morning to you, Dan," says the spiteful little old blackguard, when he saw me cleanly falling down with a bit of the handle in my hand; 'I thank you for your visit, and fair weather after you, Daniel.' I had not time to make any answer to him, for I was tumbling over and over, and rolling and rolling, at the rate of a fox-hunt. 'God help me!' says I, 'but this is a pretty pickle for a decent man to be seen in at this time of night: I am now sold fairly.' The word was not out of my mouth when, whiz! what should fly by close to my ear but a flock of wild geese, all the way from my own bog of Ballyasheenogh, else how should they know *me*? The *ould* gander, who was their general, turning about his head, cried out to me, 'Is that you, Dan?' 'The same,' said I, not a bit daunted now at what he said, for I was by this time used to all kinds of *bedevilment*, and, besides, I knew him of *ould*. 'Good morning to you,' says he, 'Daniel O'Rourke; how are you in health this morning?' 'Very well, sir,' says I, 'I thank you kindly.' drawing my breath, for I was mightily in want of some. 'I hope your honour's the same.' 'I think 'tis falling you are, Daniel,' says he. 'You may say that, sir,' says I. 'And where are you going all the way so fast?' said the gander. So I told him how I had taken the drop, and how I came on the island, and how I lost my way in the bog, and how the thief of an eagle flew me up to the moon, and how the man in the moon turned me out. 'Dan,' said he, 'I'll save you: put out your hand and catch me by the leg, and I'll fly you home.' 'Sweet is your hand in a pitcher of honey, my jewel,' says I, though all the time I thought within myself that I don't much trust you; but there was no help, so I caught the gander by the leg, and away I and the other geese flew after him as fast as hops.

"We flew, and we flew, and we flew, until we came right over the wide ocean. I knew it well, for I saw Cape Clear to my right hand, sticking up out of the water. 'Ah, my lord,' said I to the goose, for I thought it best to keep a civil tongue in my head any way, 'fly to land if you please.' 'It is impossible, you see, Dan,' said he, 'for a while, because you see we are going to Arabia.' 'To Arabia!' said I; 'that's surely some place in foreign parts, far away. Oh! Mr. Goose: why then, to be sure, I'm a man to be pitied among you.' 'Whist, whist, you fool,' said he, 'hold your tongue; I tell you Arabia is a very decent sort of place, as like West Carbery as one egg is like another, only there is a little more sand there.'

"Just as we were talking, a ship hove in sight, scudding so beautiful before the wind. 'Ah! then, sir, said I, 'will you drop me on the ship, if you please?' 'We are not fair over it,' said he; 'if I dropped you now you would go splash into the sea.' 'I would not,' says I; 'I know better than that, for it is just clean under us, so let me drop now at once.'

" 'If you must, you must,' said he; 'there, take your own way;' and he opened his claw, and faith he was right—sure enough I came down plump into the very bottom of the salt sea! Down to the very bottom I went, and I gave myself up then for ever, when a whale walked up to me, scratching himself after his night's sleep, and looked me full in the face, and never the word did he say, but lifting up his tail, he splashed me all over again with the cold salt water till there wasn't a dry stitch upon my whole carcass! and I heard somebody saying—'twas a voice I knew, too—'Get up, you drunken brute, off o' that;' and with that I woke up, and there was Judy with a tub full of water, which she was splashing all over me—for, rest her soul! though she was a good wife, she never could bear to see me in drink, and had a bitter hand of her own.

" 'Get up,' said she again: 'and of all places in the parish would no place sarve your turn to lie down upon but under the *ould* walls of the Carrigapooka? an uneasy resting I am sure you had of it.' And sure enough I had: for I was fairly bothered out of my senses with eagles, and men of the moons, and flying ganders, and whales, driving me through bogs, and up to the moon, and down to the bottom of the green ocean. If I was in drink ten times over, long would it be before I'd lie down in the same spot again, I know that."

The Kildare Pooka
Patrick Kennedy

Mr. H——— R———, when he was alive, used to live a good deal in Dublin, and he was once a great while out of the country on account of the "ninety-eight" business. But the servants kept on in the big house at Rath— all the same as if the family was at home. Well, they used to be frightened out of their lives after going to their beds with the banging of the kitchen-door, and the clattering of fire-irons, and the pots and plates and dishes. One evening they sat up ever so long, keeping one another in heart with telling stories about ghosts and fetches, and that when—what would you have of it?—the little scullery boy that used to be sleeping over the horses, and could not get room at the fire, crept into the hot hearth, and when he got tired listening to the stories, sorra fear him, but he fell dead asleep.

Well and good, after they were all gone and the kitchen fire raked up, he was woke with the noise of the kitchen door opening, and the trampling of an ass on the kitchen floor. He peeped out, and what should he see but a big ass, sure enough, sitting on his curabingo and yawning before the fire. After a little he looked about him, and began scratching his ears as if he was quite tired, and says he, "I may as well begin first as last." The poor boy's teeth began to chatter in his head, for says he, "Now he's goin' to ate me;" but the fellow with the long ears and tail on him had something else to do. He stirred the fire, and then he brought in a pail of water from the pump, and filled a big pot on the fire before he went out. He then put in his hand—foot, I mean—into the hot hearth, and pulled out the little boy. He let a roar out of him with the fright, but the pooka only looked at him, and thrust out his lower lip to show how little he valued him, and then he pitched him into his pew again.

Well, he then lay down before the fire till he heard the boil coming on the water, and maybe there wasn't a plate, or a dish, or a spoon on the dresser that he didn't fetch and put into the pot, and wash and dry the whole bilin' of 'em as well as e'er a kitchen-maid from that to Dublin town. He then put all of them up on their places on the shelves; and if he didn't give a good sweepin' to the kitchen, leave it till again. Then he comes and sits fornent the boy, let down one of his ears, and cocked up the other, and gave a grin. The poor fellow strove to roar out, but not a dheeg 'ud come out of his throat. The last thing the pooka done was to rake up the fire, and walk out, giving such a slap o' the door, that the boy thought the house couldn't help tumbling down.

Well, to be sure if there wasn't a hullabullo next morning when the poor fellow told his story! They could talk of nothing else the whole day. One said one thing, another said another, but a fat, lazy scullery girl said the wittiest thing of all. "Musha!" says she, "if the pooka does be cleaning up everything that way when we are asleep, what should we be slaving ourselves for doing his work?" "*Shu gu dheine*,"* says another; "them's the wisest words you ever said, Kauth; it's meeself won't contradict you."

So said, so done. Not a bit of a plate or dish saw a drop of water that evening, and not a besom was laid on the floor, and every one went to bed soon after sundown. Next morning everything was as fine as fine in the kitchen, and the lord mayor might eat his dinner off the flags. It was great ease to the lazy servants, you may depend, and everything went on well till a foolhardy gag of a boy said he would stay up one

---

Meant for seadh go deimhin — i.e., yes, indeed.

night and have a chat with the pooka.

He was a little daunted when the door was thrown open and the ass marched up to the fire.

"An then, sir," says he, at last, picking up courage, "if it isn't taking a liberty, might I ax who you are, and why you are so kind as to do half of the day's work for the girls every night?" "No liberty at all," says the pooka, says he: "I'll tell you, and welcome. I was a servant in the time of Squire R.'s father, and was the laziest rogue that ever was clothed and fed, and done nothing for it. When my time came for the other world, this is the punishment was laid on me—to come here and do all this labour every night, and then go out in the cold. It isn't so bad in the fine weather; but if you only knew what it is to stand with your head between your legs, facing the storm, from midnight to sunrise, on a bleak winter night." "And could we do anything for your comfort, my poor fellow?" says the boy. "Musha, I don't know," says the pooka; "but I think a good quilted frieze coat would help to keep the life in me them long nights." "Why then, in troth, we'd be the ungratefullest of people if we didn't feel for you."

To make a long story short, the next night but two the boy was there again; and if he didn't delight the poor pooka, holding up a fine warm coat before him, it's no mather! Betune the pooka and the man, his legs was got into the four arms of it, and it was buttoned down the breast and the belly, and he was so pleazed he walked up to the glass to see how he looked. "Well," says he, "it's a long lane that has no turning. I am much obliged to you and your fellow-servants. You have made me happy at last. Good-night to you."

So he was walking out, but the other cried, "Och! sure your going too soon. What about the washing and sweeping?" "Ah, you may tell the girls that they must now get their turn. My punishment was to last till I was thought worthy of a reward for the way I done my duty. You'll see me no more." And no more they did, and right sorry they were for having been in such a hurry to reward the ungrateful pooka.

How Thomas Connolly
Met the Banshee

J. Todhunter

Aw, the banshee, sir? Well, sir, as I was striving to tell ye, I was going home from work one day, from Mr. Cassidy's that I tould ye of, in the dusk o' the evening. I had more nor a mile—aye, it was nearer two mile—to thrack to, where I was lodgin' with a dacent widdy woman I knew, Biddy Maguire be name, so as to be near me work.

It was the first week in November, an' a lonesome road I had to travel, an' dark enough, wid threes above it; an' about half-ways there was a bit of a brudge I had to cross, over one o' them little sthrames that runs into the Doddher. I walked on in the middle iv the road, for there was no toe-path at that time, Misther Harry, nor for many a long day afther that; but, as I was sayin', I walked along till I come nigh upon the bridge, where the road was a bit open, an' there, right enough, I seen the hog's back o' the ould-fashioned brudge that used to be there till it was pulled down, an' a white mist steamin' up out o' the wather all around it.

Well, now, Misther Harry, often as I'd passed by the place before, that night it seemed strhrange to me, an' like a place ye might see in a dhrame; an' as I come up to it I began to feel a cowld wind blowin' through the hollow o' me heart. "Musha Thomas," sez I to meself, "is it yerself that's in it?" sez I; "or, if it is, what's the matter wid ye at all, at all?" sez I; so I put a bould face on it, an' I made a sthruggle to set one leg afore the other, ontil I came to the rise o' the brudge. And there, God be good to us! in a cantle o' the wall I seen an ould woman, as I thought, sittin' on her hunkers, all crouched together, an' her head bowed down, seemin'ly in the greatest affliction.

Well, sir, I pities the ould craythur, an' thought I wasn't worth a thraneen, for the mortial fright I was in, I up an' sez to her, "That's a cowld lodgin' for ye, ma'am." Well, the sorra ha'porth she sez to that, nor tuk no more notice o' me than if I hadn't let a word out o' me, but kep' rockin' herself to an' fro, as if her heart was breakin'; so I sez to her again, "Eh, ma'am,

is there anythin' the matther wid ye?" An' I made for to touch
her on the shouldher, on'y somethin' stopt me, for as I looked
closer at her I saw she was no more an ould woman nor was
she an ould cat. The first thing I tuk notice to, Misther Harry,
was her hair, that was sthreelin' down over his showldhers,
an' a good yard on the ground on aich side of her. O, be the
hoky farmer, but that was the hair! The likes of it I never seen
on mortial woman, young or ould, before nor sense. It grew as
sthrong out of her as out of e'er a young slip of a girl ye could
see; but the colour of it was a misthery to describe. The first
squint I got of it I thought it was silvery grey, like an ould
crone's; but when I got up beside her I saw, be the glance o'
the sky, it was a soart iv an Iscariot colour, an' a shine out of it
like floss silk. It ran over her showldhers and the two shapely
arms she was lanin' her hed on, for all the world like Mary
Magdalen's in a picther; and then I persaved that the grey
cloak and the green gownd undhernaith it was made of no
earthly mataril I ever laid eyes on. Now, I needn't tell ye, sir,
that I seen all this in the twinkle of a bed-post— long as I take
to make the narration of it. So I made a step back from her, an'
"The Lord be betune us an' harm!" sez I, out loud, an' wid that
I blessed meself. Well, Misther Harry, the word wasn't out o'
me mouth afore she turned her face on me. Aw, Misther Harry,
but 'twas that was the awfullest apparition ever I seen, the
face of her as she looked up at me! God forgive me for sayin'

it, but 'twas more like the face of the "Axy Homo" bezand in Marlboro' Sthreet Chapel nor like any face I could mintion— as pale as a corpse, an' a most o' freckles on it, like the freckles on a turkey's egg; an' the two eyes sewn in wid red thread, from the terrible power o' crying the' had to do; and such a pair iv eyes as the' wor, Misther Harry, as blue as two forget-me-nots, an' as cowld as the moon in a bog-hole of a frosty night, an' a dead-an'-live look in them that sent cowld shiver through the marra o' me bones. Be the mortial! ye could ha' rung a tay cupful o' cowld paspiration out o' the hair o' me head that minute, so ye could. Well, I thought the life 'ud leve me intirely when she riz up from her hunkers, till, bedad! she looked mostly as tall as Nelson's Pillar; an' wid the two eyes gazin' back at me, an' her two arms stretched out before hor, an' a keine out of her that riz the hair o' me scalp till it was as stiff as the hog's bristles in a new hearth broom, away she glides—glides round the angle o' the brudge, an' down with her into the sthrame that ran undhernaith it. 'Twas then I began to suspect what she was. "Wisha, Thomas!" says I to meself, sez I; an' I made a great struggle to get me two legs into a throt, in spite o' the spavin o' fright the pair o' them wor in; an' how I brought meself home that same night the Lord in heaven only knows, for I never could tell; but I must ha' tumbled again the door, and shot in head foremost into the middle o' the flure, where I lay in a deadswoon for mostly an hour;

and the first I knew was Mrs. Maguire stannin' over me with a jorum o' punch she was pourin' down me throath, to bring back the life into me, an' me head in a pool of cowld wather she dashed over me in her first fright. "Arrah, Mister Connolly," shashee, "what ails ye?" shashee, "to put the scare on a lone woman like that?" shashee. "Am I in this world or the next?" sez I. "Musha! where else would ye be on'y here in my kitchen?" shashee. "O, glory be to God!" sez I, "but I thought I was in Purgathory at the laste, not to mintion an uglier place," sez I, "only it's too cowld I find meself, an' not too hot," sez I. "Faix, an' maybe ye wor more nor half-ways there, on'y for me," shashee; "but what's come to you at all, at all? Is it your fetch ye seen, Mister Connolly?" "Aw, naboclish!"* sez I. "Never mind what I seen," sez I. So be degrees I began to come to a little; an' that's the way I met the banshee, Misther Harry!

"But how did you know it really was the banshee after all, Thomas?"

"Begor, sir, I knew the apparation of her well enough; but 'twas confirmed by a sarcumstance that occurred the same time. There was a Misther O'Nales was come on a visit, ye must know, to a place in the neighbourhood— one o' the ould O'Nales iv the county Tyrone, a rale ould Irish family—

---

*Na bac leis -- i.e., don't mind it.

an' the banshee was heard keening round the house that same night, be more then one that was in it; an' sure enough, Misther Harry, he was found dead in his bed the next mornin'. So if it wasn't the banshee I seen that time, I'd like to know what else it could a' been."

The Legend of Knocksheogowna

T. Crofton Croker

In Tipperary is one of the most singularly shaped hills in the world. It has got a peak at the top like a conical nightcap thrown carelessly over your head as you awake in the morning. On the very point is built a sort of lodge, where, in the summer, the lady who built it and her friends used to go on parties of pleasure; but that was long after the days of the fairies, and it is, I believe, now deserted.

But before lodge was built, or acre sown, there was close to the head of this hill a large pasturage, where a herdsman spent his days and nights among the herd. The spot had been an old fairy ground, and the good people were angry that the scene of their light and airy gambols should be trampled by the rude hoofs of bulls and cows. The lowing of the cattle sounded sad in their ears, and the chief of the fairies of the hill determined in person to drive away the new-comers; and the way she thought of was this: When the harvest nights came on, and the moon shone bright and brilliant over the hill, and the cattle were lying down hushed and quiet, and the herds-man, wrapt in his mantle, was musing with his heart glad-dened by the glorious company of the stars twinkling above him, she would come and dance before him—now in one shape, now in another—but all ugly and frightful to behold. One time she would be a great horse, with the wings of an eagle and a tail like a dragon, hissing loud and spitting fire. Then, in a moment, she would change into a little man lame of a leg, with a bull's head, and a lambent flame playing round it. Then into a great ape, with duck's feet and a turkey-cock's tail. But I should be all day about it were I to tell you all the shapes she took. And then she would roar, or neigh, or hiss, or bellow, or howl, or hoot, as never yet was roaring, neighing, hissing, bellowing, howling, or hooting heard in the world before or since. The poor herdsman would cover his face, and call on all the saints for help, but it was no use. With one puff of her breath she would blow away the fold of his great-coat, let him hold it ever so tightly over his eyes, and not a saint in heaven paid him the slightest attention. And to make matters worse, he never could stir; no, nor even shut his eyes, but there was obliged to stay, held by what power he knew not, gazing at these terrible sights until the hair of his head would lift his hat half a foot over his crown, and his teeth would be ready to fall out from chattering. But the cattle would scamper about mad, as if they were bitten by the fly; and this would last until the sun rose over the hill.

The poor cattle, from want of rest, were pining away, and food did them no good; besides, they met with accidents without end. Never a night passed that some of them did not fall into a pit, and get maimed, or maybe killed. Some would tumble into a river and be drowned; in a word, there seemed never to be an end of the accidents. But what made the matter worse, there could not be a herdsman got to tend the cattle by night. One visit from the fairy drove the stoutest-hearted almost mad. The owner of the ground did not know what to do. He offered double, treble, quadruple wages, but not a man could be found for the sake of money to go through the horror of facing the fairy. She rejoiced at the successful issue of her project, and continued her pranks. The herd gradually thinning, and no man daring to remain on the ground, the fairies came back in numbers, and gambolled as merrily as before, quaffing dew-drops from acorns, and spreading their feast on the heads of capacious mushrooms.

What was to be done? The puzzled farmer thought in

vain. He found that his substance was daily diminishing, his people terrified, and his rent-day coming round. It is no wonder that he looked gloomy, and walked mournfully down the road. Now in that part of the world dwelt a man of the name of Larry Hoolahan, who played on the pipes better than any other player within fifteen parishes. A roving, dashing blade was Larry, and feared nothing. Give him plenty of liquor, and he would defy the devil. He would face a mad bull, or fight single-handed against a fair. In one of his gloomy walks, the farmer met him, and on Larry's asking the cause of his down looks, he told him all his misfortunes.

"If that is all ails you," said Larry, "make your mind easy. Were there as many fairies on Knocksheogowna as there are potato-blossoms in Eliogurty, I would face them. It would be a queer thing, indeed, if I, who never was afraid of a proper man, should turn my back upon a brat of a fairy not the bigness of one's thumb.

"Larry," said the farmer, "do not talk so bold, for you know not who is hearing you; but if you make your words good, and watch my herds for a week on the top of the mountain, your hand shall be free of my dish till the sun has burnt itself down to the bigness of a farthing rushlight."

The bargain was struck, and Larry went to the hill-top, when the moon began to peep over the brow. He had been regaled at the farmer's house, and was bold with the extract of barley-corn. So he took his seat on a big stone under a hollow of the hill, with his back to the wind, and pulled out his pipes. He had not played long when the voice of the fairies was heard upon the blast, like a slow stream of music. Presently they burst out into a loud laugh, and Larry could plainly hear one say: "What! Another man upon the fairies'ring? Go to him, queen, and make him repent his rashness;" and they flew away. Larry felt them pass by his face as they flew, like a swarm of midgies; and looking up hastily, he saw, between the moon and him, a great black cat, standing on the very tip of its claws, with its back up, and mewing with the voice of a water-mill. Presently it swelled up towards the sky, and turning round on its left hind-leg, whirled till it fell to the ground, from which it started up in the shape of a salmon, with a cravat round its neck, and a pair of new top-boots.

　　"Go on, jewel," said Larry. "If you dance, I'll pipe," and he struck up. So she turned into this and that and the other, but still Larry played on, as he well knew how. At last she lost patience, as ladies will do when you do not mind their scold-ing, and changed herself into a calf, milk-white as the cream of Cork, and with eyes as mild as those of the girl I love. She came up gentle and fawning, in hopes to throw him off his guard by quietness, and then to work him some wrong. But Larry was not so deceived; for when she came up, he, drop-ping his pipes, leaped upon her back.

153

Now from the top of Knocksheogowna, as you look westward to the broad Atlantic, you will see the Shannon, queen of rivers, "spreading like a sea," and running on in gentle course to mingle with the ocean through the fair city of Limerick. It on this night shone under the moon, and looked beautiful from the distant hill. Fifty boats were gliding up and down on the sweet current, and the song of the fishermen rose gaily from the shore. Larry, as I said before, leaped upon the back of the fairy, and she, rejoiced at the opportunity, sprung from the hill-top, and bounded clear, at one jump, over the Shannon, flowing as it was just ten miles from the mountain's base. It was done in a second, and when she alighted on the distant bank, kicking up her heels, she flung Larry on the soft turf. No sooner was he thus planted, than he looked her straight in the face, and scratching his head, cried out: "By my word, well done! That was not a bad leap for a calf!"

She looked at him for a moment, and then assumed her own shape. "Laurence," said she, "you are a bold fellow. Will you come back the way you went?"

"And that's what I will," said he, "if you let me." So changing to a calf again, again Larry got on her back, and at another bound, they were again upon the top of Knocksheogowna. The fairy, once more resuming her figure, addressed him:

"You have shown so much courage, Laurence," said

she, "that while you keep herds on this hill you never shall be molested by me or mine. The day dawns; go down to the farmer and tell him this, and if anything I can do may be of service to you, ask, and you shall have it."

She vanished accordingly, and kept her word in never visiting the hill during Larry's life; but he never troubled her with requests. He piped and drank at the farmer's expense, and roosted in his chimney-corner, occasionally casting an eye to the flock. He died at last, and is buried in a green valley of pleasant Tipperary; but whether the fairies returned to the hill of Knocksheogowna after his death, is more than I can say.

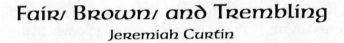

Fairy Browny and Trembling
Jeremiah Curtin

King Aedh Curucha lived in Tir Conal, and he had three daughters, whose names were Fair, Brown, and Trembling.

Fair and Brown had new dresses, and went to church every Sunday. Trembling was kept at home to do the cooking and work. They would not let her go out of the house at all; for she was more beautiful than the other two, and they were in dread she might marry before themselves.

They carried on in this way for seven years. At the end of seven years the son of the king of Omanya fell in love with the eldest sister.

One Sunday morning, after the other two had gone to

church, the old henwife came into the kitchen to Trembling, and said: "It's at church you ought to be this day, instead of working here at home."

"How could I go?" said Trembling. "I have no clothes good enough to wear at church; and if my sisters were to see me there, they'd kill me for going out of the house."

"I'll give you," said the henwife, "a finer dress than either of them has ever seen. And now tell me what dress will you have?"

"I'll have," said Trembling, " a dress as white as snow, and green shoes for my feet."

Then the henwife put on the cloak of darkness, clipped a piece from the old clothes the young woman had on, and asked for the whitest robes in the world and the most beautiful that could be found, and a pair of green shoes.

That moment she had the robe and the shoes, and she brought them to Trembling, who put them on. When Trembling was dressed and ready, the henwife said: "I have a honey-bird here to sit on your right shoulder, and a honey-finger to put on your left. At the door stands a milk-white mare, with a golden saddle for you to sit on, and a golden bridle to hold in your hand."

Trembling sat on the golden saddle; and when she was ready to start, the henwife said: "You must not go inside the door of the church, and the minute the people rise up at the

157

end of Mass, do you make off, and ride home as fast as the mare will carry you."

When Trembling came to the door of the church there was no one inside who could get a glimpse of her but was striving to know who she was; and when they saw her hurrying away at the end of Mass, they ran out to overtake her. But no use in their running; she was away before any man could come near her. From the minute she left the church till she got home, she overtook the wind before her, and outstripped the wind behind.

She came down at the door, went in, and found the henwife had dinner ready. She put off the white robes, and had on her old dress in a twinkling.

When the two sisters came home the henwife asked: "Have you any news to-day from the church?"

"We have great news," said they. "We saw a wonderful, grand lady at the church-door. The like of the robes she had we have never seen on woman before. It's little that was thought of our dresses beside what she had on; and there was n't a man at the church, from the king to the beggar, but was trying to look at her and know who she was."

The sisters would give no peace till they had two dresses like the robes of the strange lady; but honey-birds and honey-fingers were not to be found.

Next Sunday the two sisters went to church again, and

left the youngest at home to cook the dinner.

After they had gone, the henwife came in and asked: "Will you go to church to-day?"

"I would go," said Trembling, "if I could get the going."

"What robe will you wear?" asked the henwife.

"The finest black satin that can be found, and red shoes for my feet."

"What color do you want the mare to be?"

"I want her to be so black and so glossy that I can see myself in her body."

The henwife put on the cloak of darkness, and asked for the robes and the mare. That moment she had them. When trembling was dressed, the henwife put the honey-bird on her right shoulder and the honey-finger on her left. The saddle on the mare was silver, and so was the bridle.

When Trembling sat in the saddle and was going away, the henwife ordered her strictly not to go inside the door of the church, but to rush away as soon as the people rose at the end of Mass, and hurry home on the mare before any man could stop her.

That Sunday the people were more astonished than ever, and gazed at her more than the first time; and all they were thinking of was to know who she was. But they had no chance; for the moment the people rose at the end of Mass she slipped from the church, was in the silver saddle, and home before a man could stop her or talk to her.

The henwife had the dinner ready. Trembling took off her satin robe, and had on her old clothes before her sisters got home.

"What news have you to-day?" asked the henwife of the sisters when they came from the church.

"Oh, we saw the grand strange lady again! And it's little that any man could think of our dresses after looking at the robes of satin that she had on! And all at church, from high to low, had their mouths open, gazing at her, and no man was looking at us."

The two sisters gave neither rest nor peace till they got dresses as nearly like the strange lady's robes as they could find. Of course they were not so good; for the like of those robes could not be found in Erin.

When the third Sundy came, Fair and Brown went to church dressed in black satin. They left Trembling at home to work in the kitchen, and told her to be sure and have dinner ready when they came back.

After they had gone and were out of sight, the henwife came to the kitchen and said: "Well, my dear, are you for church to-day?"

"I would go if I had a new dress to wear."

"I'll get you any dress you ask for. What dress would you like?" asked the henwife.

"A dress red as a rose from the waist down, and white as snow from the waist up; a cape of green on my shoulders; and a hat on my head with a red, a white, and a green feather in it; and shoes for my feet with the toes red, the middle white, and the backs and heels green."

The henwife put on the cloak of darkness, wished for all these things, and had them. When Trembling was dressed, the henwife put the honey-bird on her right shoulder and the honey-finger on her left, and placing the hat on her head, clipped a few hairs from one lock and a few from another with her scissors, and that moment the most beautiful golden hair was flowing down over the girl's shoulders. Then the henwife asked what kind of mare she would ride. She said white, with blue-and gold-colored diamond-shaped spots all over her body, on her back a saddle of gold, and on her head a golden bridle.

The mare stood there before the door, and a bird sitting between her ears, which began to sing as soon as Trembling was in the saddle, and never stopped till she came home from the church.

The fame of the beautiful strange lady had gone out through the world, and all the princes and great men that were in it came to church that Sunday, each one hoping that it was himself would have her home with him after Mass.

The son of the king of Omanya forgot all about the eldest sister, and remained outside the church, so as to catch the strange lady before she could hurry away.

The church was more crowded than ever before, and there were three times as many outside. There was such a throng before the church that Trembling could only come inside the gate.

As soon as the people were rising at the end of Mass, the lady slipped out through the gate, was in the golden saddle in an instant, and sweeping away ahead of the wind. But if she was, the prince of Omanya was at her side, and, seizing her by the foot, he ran with the mare for thirty paces, and never let go of the beautiful lady till the shoe was pulled from her foot, and he was left behind with it in his hand. She came home as fast as the mare could carry her, and was thinking all the time that the henwife would kill her for losing the shoe.

Seeing her so vexed and so changed in the face, the old woman asked: "What's the trouble that's on you now?"

"Oh! I've lost one of the shoes off my feet," said Trembling.

"Don't mind that; don't be vexed," said the henwife; "maybe it's the best thing that ever happened to you."

Then Trembling gave up all the things she had to the henwife, put on her old clothes, and went to work in the kitchen. When the sisters came home, the henwife asked: "Have you any news from the church?"

"We have indeed," said they; "for we saw the grandest sight to-day. The strange lady came again, in grander array than before. On herself and the horse she rode were the finest colors of the world, and between the ears of the horse was a bird which never stopped singing from the time she came till she went away. The lady herself is the most beautiful woman ever seen by man in Erin."

After Trembling had disappeared from the church, the son of the king of Omanya said to the other kings' sons: "I will have that lady for my own."

They all said: "You did n't win her just by taking the shoe off her foot, you'll have to win her by the point of your sword; you'll have to fight for her with us before you can call her your own."

"Well," said the son of the king of Omanya, "when I find the lady that shoe will fit, I'll fight for her, never fear, before I leave her to any of you."

Then all the kings' sons were uneasy, and anxious to know who was she that lost the shoe; and they began to travel all over Erin to know could they find her. The prince of Omanya and all the others went in a great company together, and made the round of Erin; they went everywhere—north, south, east, and west. They visited every place where a woman was to be found, and left not a house in the kingdom they did not search, to know could they find the woman the shoe would fit, not caring whether she was rich or poor, of high or low degree.

The prince of Omanya always kept the shoe; and when the young women saw it, they had great hopes, for it was of proper size, neither large nor small, and it would beat any man to know of what material it was made. One thought it would fit her if she cut a little from her great toe; and another, with too short a foot, put something in the tip of her stocking. But no use, they only spoiled their feet, and were curing them for months afterwards.

The two sisters, Fair and Brown, heard that the princes of the world were looking all over Erin for the woman that could wear the shoe, and every day they were talking of trying it on; and one day Trembling spoke up and said: "Maybe it's my foot that the shoe will fit."

"Oh, the breaking of the dog's foot on you! Why say so when you were at home every Sunday?"

They were that way waiting, and scolding the younger sister, till the princes were near the place. The day they were to come, the sisters put Trembling in a closet, and locked the door on her. When the company came to the house, the prince of Omanya gave the shoe to the sisters. But though they tried and tried, it would fit neither of them.

"Is there any other young woman in the house?" asked the prince.

"There is," said Trembling, speaking up in the closet; "I'm here."

"Oh! we have her for nothing but to put out the ashes," said the sisters.

But the prince and the others would n't leave the house till they had seen her; so the two sisters had to open the door. When Trembling came out, the shoe was given to her, and it fitted exactly.

The prince of Omanya looked at her and said: "You are the woman the shoe fits, and you are the woman I took the shoe from."

Then Trembling spoke up, and said: "Do you stay here till I return."

Then she went to the henwife's house. The old woman put on the cloak of darkness, got everything for her she had the first Sunday at church, and put her on the white mare in the same fashion. Then Trembling rode along the highway to the front of the house. All who saw her the first time said: "This is the lady we saw at church."

Then she went away a second time, and a second time came back on the black mare in the second dress which the henwife gave her. All who saw her the second Sunday said: "That is the lady we saw at church."

A third time she asked for a short absence, and soon came back on the third mare and in the third dress. All who saw her the third time said: "This is the lady we saw at church." Every man was satisfied, and knew that she was the woman.

Then all the princes and great men spoke up, and said to the son of the king of Omanya: "You'll have to fight now for her before we let her go with you."

"I'm here before you, ready for combat," answered the prince.

Then the son of the king of Lochlin stepped forth. The struggle began, and a terrible struggle it was. They fought for nine hours; and then the son of the king of Lochlin stopped, gave up his claim, and left the field. Next day the son of the king of Spain fought six hours, and yielded his claim. On the third day the son of the king of Nyerfoi fought eight hours, and stopped. The fourth day the son of the king of Greece fought six hours, and stopped. On the fifth day no more strange princes wanted to fight; and all the sons of kings in Erin said they would not fight with a man of their own land, that the strangers had had their chance, and as no others came to claim the woman, she belonged of right to the son of the king of Omanya.

The marriage-day was fixed, and the invitations were sent out. The wedding lasted for a year and a day. When the wedding was over, the king's son brought home the bride, and when the time came a son was born. The young woman sent for her eldest sister, Fair, to be with her and care for her. One day, when Trembling was well, and when her husband was away hunting, the two sisters went out to walk; and when they came to the seaside, the eldest pushed the youngest sister in. A great whale came and swallowed her.

The eldest sister came home alone, and the husband asked, "Where is your sister?"

"She has gone home to her father in Ballyshannon; now that I am well, I don't need her."

"Well," said the husband, looking at her, "I'm in dread it's my wife that has gone."

"Oh! no," said she; "it's my sister Fair that's gone."

Since the sisters were very much alike, the prince was in doubt. That night he put his sword between them, and said: "If you are my wife, this sword will get warm; if not, it will stay cold."

In the morning when he rose up, the sword was as cold as when he put it there.

It happened that when the two sisters were walking by the seashore, that a little cowboy was down by the water minding cattle, and saw Fair push Trembling into the sea; and next day, when the tide came in, he saw the whale swim up and throw her out on the sand. When she was on the sand she said to the cowboy: "When you go home in the evening with the cows, tell the master that my sister Fair pushed me into the sea yesterday; that a whale swallowed me, and then threw me out, but will come again and swallow me with the coming of

167

the next tide; then he'll go out with the tide, and come again with to-morrow's tide, and throw me again on the strand. The whale will cast me out three times. I'm under the enchantment of this whale, and cannot leave the beach or escape myself. Unless my husband saves me before I'm swallowed the fourth time, I shall be lost. He must come and shoot the whale with a silver bullet when he turns on the broad of his back. Under the breast-fin of the whale is a reddish-brown spot. My husband must hit him in that spot, for it is the only place in which he can be killed."

When the cowboy got home, the eldest sister gave him a draught of oblivion, and he did not tell.

Next day he went again to the sea. The whale came and cast Trembling on shore again. She asked the boy: "Did you tell the master what I told you to tell him?"

"I did not," said he; "I forgot."

"How did you forget?" asked she.

"The woman of the house gave me a drink that made me forget."

"Well, don't forget telling him this night; and if she gives you a drink, don't take it from her."

As soon as the cowboy came home, the eldest sister offered him a drink. He refused to take it till he had delivered his message and told all to the master. The third day the prince went down with his gun and a silver bullet in it. He was not long down when the whale came out and threw Trembling upon the beach as the two days before. She had no power to speak to her husband till he had killed the whale. Then the whale went out, turned over once on the broad of his back, and showed the spot for a moment only. That moment the prince fired. He had but the one chance, and a short one at that; but he took it, and hit the spot, and the whale, mad with pain, made the sea all around red with blood, and died.

That minute Trembling was able to speak, and went home with her husband, who sent word to her father what the eldest sister had done. The father came, and told him any death he chose to give her to give it. The prince told the father he would leave her life and death with himself. The father had her put out then on the sea in a barrel, with provisions in it for seven years.

In time Trembling had a second child, a daughter. The prince and she sent the cowboy to school, and trained him up as one of their own children, and said: "If the little girl that is born to us now lives, no other man in the world will get her but him."

The cowboy and the prince's daughter lived on till they were married. The mother said to her husband: "You could not have saved me from the whale but for the little cowboy; on that account I don't grudge him my daughter."

The son of the king of Omanya and Trembling had fourteen children, and they lived happily till the two died of old age.

Legend of Bottle Hill
T. Crofton Croker

It was in the good days, when the little people, most impudently called fairies, were more frequently seen than they are in these unbelieving times, that a farmer, named Mick Purcell, rented a few acres of barren ground in the neighbourhood of the once celebrated preceptory of Mourne, situated about three miles from Mallow and thirteen from "the beautiful city called Cork." Mick had a wife and family: they all did what they could, and that was but little, for the poor man had no child grown up big enough to help him in his work; and all the poor woman could do was to mind the children, and to milk the one cow, and to boil the potatoes, and to carry the eggs to market to Mallow; but with all they could do, 'twas hard enough on them to pay the rent. Well, they did manage it for a good while; but at last came a bad year, and the little grain of oats was all spilled, and the chickens died of the pip, and the pig got the measles—she was sold in Mallow and brought almost nothing; and poor Mick found that he hadn't enough to half pay his rent, and two gales were due.

"Why, then, Molly," says he, "what'll we do?"

"Wisha, then, mavourneen, what would you do but take the cow to the fair of Cork and sell her?" says she. "And Monday is fair day, and so you must go to-morrow, that the poor beast may be rested again at the fair."

"And what'll we do when she's gone?" says Mick sorrowfully.

"Never a know I know, Mick; but sure, God won't leave us without Him, Mick; and you know how good He was to us when poor little Billy was sick, and we had nothing at all for him to take, that good doctor gentleman at Ballydahin come riding and asking for a drink of milk; and how he gave us two shillings; and how he sent the things and bottles for the child, and gave me my breakfast when I went over to ask a question, so he did; and how he came to see Billy, and never left off his goodness till he was quite well?"

"Oh, you are always that way, Molly, and I believe you are right, after all, so I won't be sorry for selling the cow; but I'll go to-morrow, and you must put a needle and thread through my coat, for you know 'tis ripped under the arm."

Molly told him he should have everything right; and about twelve o'clock next day he left her, getting a charge not to sell his cow except for the highest penny. Mick promised to mind it, and went his way along the road. He drove his cow slowly through the little stream which crosses it, and runs by the old walls of Mourne. As he passed he glanced his eye upon the towers and one of the old elder trees, which were only then little bits of switches.

"Oh, then, if I only had half the money that's buried in you, 'tisn't driving this poor cow I'd be now! Why, then, isn't it too bad that it should be there covered over with earth, and many a one besides me wanting? Well, if it's God's will, I'll have some money myself coming back."

So saying, he moved on after his beast. 'Twas a fine day, and the sun shone brightly on the walls of the old abbey as he passed under them; he then crossed an extensive mountain track, and after six long miles, he came to the top of that hill – Bottle Hill 'tis called now, but that was not the name of it then, and just there a man overtook him. "Good morrow!" says he.

"Good morrow!" kindly says Mick, looking at the stranger, who was a little man, you'd almost call him a dwarf, only he wasn't quite so little neither; he had a bit of an old, wrinkled, yellow face, for all the world like a dried cauliflower, only he had a sharp little nose, and red eyes and white hair, and his lips were not red, but all his face was one colour, and his eyes never were quiet, but looking at everything, and although they were red, they made Mick feel quite cold when he looked at them. In truth, he did not much like the little man's company; and he couldn't see one bit of his legs nor his body; for, though the day was warm, he was all wrapped up in a big great-coat. Mick drove his cow something faster, but the little man kept up with him. Mick didn't know how he walked, for he was almost afraid to look at him, and to cross himself, for fear the old man would be angry. Yet he thought his fellow-traveller did not seem to walk like other men, nor to put one foot before the other, but to glide over the rough road – and rough enough it was—like a shadow, without noise and with-out effort. Mick's heart trembled within him, and he said a prayer to himself, wishing he hadn't come out that day, or that he was on Fair Hill, or that he hadn't the cow to mind, that he might run away from the bad thing—when, in the midst of his fears, he was again addressed by his companion.

"Where are you going with the cow, honest man?"

"To the fair of Cork, then," says Mick, trembling at the shrill and piercing tones of the voice.

"Are you going to sell her?" said the stranger.

"Why, then, what else am I going for but to sell her?"

"Will you sell her to me?"

Mick started – he was afraid to have anything to do with the little man, and he was more afraid to say no.

"What'll you give for her?" at last says he.

"I'll tell you what, I'll give you this bottle," said the little one, pulling a bottle from under his coat.

Mick looked at him and the bottle, and in spite of his terror, he could not help bursting into a loud fit of laughter.

"Laugh if you will," said the little man; "but I tell you this bottle is better for you than all the money you will get for the cow in Cork—ay, than ten thousand times as much."

Mick laughed again. "Why, then," says he, "do you think I am such a fool as to give my good cow for a bottle – and an empty one too? Indeed, then, I won't."

"You had better give me the cow, and take the bottle – you'll not be sorry for it."

"Why, then, and what would Molly say? I'd never hear the end of it; and how would I pay the rent? And what would we all do without a penny of money?"

"I tell you this bottle is better to you than money; take it, and give me the cow. I ask you for the last time, Mick Purcell."

Mick started.

"How does he know my name?" thought he.

The stranger proceeded: "Mick Purcell, I know you, and I have a regard for you; therefore, do as I warn you, or you may be sorry for it. How do you know but your cow will die before you get to Cork?"

Mick was going to say "God forbid!" but the little man went on (and he was too attentive to say anything to stop him; for Mick was a very civil man, and he knew better than to interrupt a gentleman, and that's what many people that hold their heads higher don't mind now).

"And how do you know but there will be much cattle at the fair, and you will get a bad price, or maybe you might be robbed when you are coming home? But what need I talk more to you, when you are determined to throw away your luck, Mick Purcell?"

"Oh, no! I would not throw away my luck, sir," said Mick. "And if I was sure the bottle was as good as you say— though I never liked an empty bottle, although I had drank what was in it— I'd give you the cow in the name—"

"Never mind names," said the stranger, "but give me the cow; I would not tell you a lie. Here, take the bottle, and when you go home do what I direct exactly."

Mick hesitated.

"Well, then, good-bye! I can stay no longer. Once more, take it, and be rich; refuse it, and beg for your life, and see your children in poverty and your wife dying for want; that will happen to you, Mick Purcell!" said the little man, with a malicious grin, which made him look ten times more ugly than

175

ever.

"Maybe 'tis true," said Mick, still hesitating; he did not know what to do – he could hardly help believing the old man, and at length, in a fit of desperation, he seized the bottle. "Take the cow," said he, "and if you are telling a lie, the curse of the poor will be on you."

"I care neither for your curses nor your blessings, but I have spoken truth, Mick Purcell, and that you will find to-night, if you do what I tell you."

"And what's that?" says Mick.

"When you go home, never mind if your wife is angry, but be quiet yourself, and make her sweep the room clean, set the table out right, and spread a clean cloth over it; then put the bottle on the ground, saying these words, 'Bottle, do your duty,' and you will see the end of it."

"And is this all?" says Mick.

"No more," said the stranger. "Good-bye, Mick Purcell! You are a rich man."

"God grant it!" said Mick, as the old man moved after the cow, and Mick retraced the road towards his cabin; but he could not help turning back to look after the purchaser of his cow, who was nowhere to be seen.

"Lord between us and harm!" said Mick. "He can't belong to this earth; but where is the cow?" She, too, was gone, and Mick went homeward muttering prayers, and holding fast the bottle.

"And what would I do if it broke?" thought he. "Oh, but I'll take care of that." So he put it into his bosom, and went on, anxious to prove his bottle, and doubting of the reception he should meet from his wife. Balancing his anxieties with his expectation, his fears with his hopes, he reached home in the evening, and surprised his wife sitting over the turf fire in the big chimney.

"Oh, Mick, are you come back? Sure, you weren't at Cork all the way? What has happened to you? Where is the cow? Did you sell her? How much money did you get for her? What news have you? Tell us everything about it."

"Why, then, Molly, if you'll give me time, I'll tell you all about it. If you want to know where the cow is, 'tisn't Mick can tell you, for the never a know does he know where she is now."

"Oh, then, you sold her. And where's the money?"

"Arrah! Stop a while, Molly, and I'll tell you all about it."

"But what is that bottle under your waistcoat?" said Molly, spying its neck sticking out.

"Why, then, be easy now, can't you," says Mick, "till I tell it to you?" and putting the bottle on the table: "That's all I got for the cow."

His poor wife was thunderstruck. "All you got! And what good is that, Mick? Oh, I never thought you were such a fool? And what'll we do for the rent, and what—"

"Now, Molly," sys Mick, "can't you hearken to reason. Didn't I tell you how the old man, or whatsomever he was, met me – no, he didn't meet me neither, but he was there with me – on the big hill, and how he made me sell him the cow, and told me the bottle was the only thing for me?"

"Yes, indeed; the only thing for you, you fool!" said Molly, seizing the bottle to hurl it at her poor husband's head; but Mick caught it, and quietly (for he minded the old man's advice) loosened his wife's grasp, and placed the bottle again in his bosom. Poor Molly sat down crying, while Mick told her his story, with many a crossing and blessing between him and harm. His wife could not help believing him, particularly as she had as much faith in fairies as she had in the priest, who indeed never discouraged her belief in the fairies; maybe he didn't know she believed in them, and maybe he believed in them himself. She got up, however, without saying one word, and began to seep the earthen floor with a bunch of heath; then she tidied up everything, and put out the long table, and spread the clean cloth, for she had only one, upon it, and Mick, placing the bottle on the ground, looked at it, and said: "Bottle, do your duty."

"Look there! Look there, mammy!" said his chubby eldest son, a boy about five years old—"look there! look there!" and he sprang to his mother's side, as two tiny little fellows rose like light from the bottle, and in an instant covered the table with dishes and plates of gold and silver, full of the finest victuals that ever were seen, and when all was done, went into the bottle again. Mick and his wife looked at everything with astonishment; they had never seen such plates and dishes before, and didn't think they could ever admire them enough; the very sight almost took away their appetites; but at length Molly said: "Come and sit down, Mick, and try and eat a bit; sure, you ought to be hungry after such a good day's work."

"Why, then, the man told no lie about the bottle."

Mick sat down, after putting the children to the table, and they made a hearty meal, though they couldn't taste half the dishes.

"Now," says Molly, "I wonder will those two good little gentlemen carry away these fine things again?" They waited, but no one came; so Molly put up the dishes and plates very carefully, saying: "Why, then, Mick, that was no lie, sure enough; but you'll be a rich man yet, Mick Purcell."

Mick and his wife and children went to their bed, not to sleep, but to settle about selling the fine things they did not want, and to take more land. Mick went to Cork and sold his plate, and bought a horse and cart, and began to show that he was making money; and they did all they could to keep the bottle a secret; but for all that, their landlord found it out, for he came to Mick one day, and asked him where he got all his money – sure, it was not by the farm; and he bothered him so much, that at last Mick told him of the bottle. His landlord offered him a deal of money for it; but Mick would not give it, till at last he offered to give him all his farm for ever; so Mick, who was very rich, thought he'd never want any more money, and gave him the bottle; but Mick was mistaken – he and his family spent money as if there was no end of it; and to make the story short, they became poorer and poorer, till at last they had nothing but one cow; and Mick once more drove his cow before him to see her at Cork's Fair, hoping to meet the old man and get another bottle. It was hardly daybreak when he left home, and he walked on at a good pace till he reached the big hill; the mists were sleeping in the valleys, and curling like smoke-wreaths upon the brown heath around him. The sun rose on his left, and just at his feet a lark sprang from its grassy couch and poured forth its joyous matin song, ascending into the clear blue sky—

> *"Till its form like a speck in the airiness blending,*
> *And thrilling with music, was melting in light."*

Mick crossed himself, listening as he advanced to the sweet song of the lark, but thinking, notwithstanding, all the time of the little old man; when, just as he reached the summit of the hill, and cast his eyes over the extensive prospect before and around him, he was startled and rejoiced by the same well-known voice: "Well, Mick Purcell, I told you you would be a rich man."

"Indeed, then, sure enough I was; that's no lie for you, sir. Good morning to you; but it is not rich I am now – but have you another bottle, for I want it now as much as I did long ago; so if you have it, sir, here is the cow for it."

"And here is the bottle," said the old man, smiling. "You know what to do with it."

"Oh, then, sure I do, as good right I have."

"Well, farewell forever, Mick Purcell! I told you you would be a rich man."

"And good-bye to you, sir," said Mick, as he turned back; "and good luck to you, and good luck to the big hill—it wants a name—Bottle Hill. Good-bye, sir, good-bye!" so Mick walked back as fast as he could, never looking after the white-faced little gentleman and the cow, so anxious was he to bring home the bottle. Well, he arrived with it safely enough, and called out, as soon as he saw Molly: "Oh, sure, I've another bottle!"

"Arrah! Then, have you? Why, then, you're a lucky man, Mick Purcell, that's what you are."

In an instant she put everything right; and Mick, look-ing at his bottle, exultingly cried out: "Bottle, do your duty." In a twinkling, two great stout men with big cudgels issued from the bottle (I do not know how they got room in it), and belaboured poor Mick and his wife and all his family, till they lay on the floor, when in they went again. Mick, as soon as he recovered, got up and looked about him; he thought and thought, and at last he took up his wife and his children; and leaving them to recover as well as they could, he took the bottle under his coat, and went to the landlord, who had a great company. He got a servant to tell him he wanted to speak to him, and at last he came out to Mick.

"Well, what do you want now?"

"Nothing, sir; only I have another bottle."

"Oh, ho! Is it as good as the first?"

"Yes, sir, and better; if you like, I will show it to you before all the ladies and gentlemen."

"Come along, then." So saying, Mick was brought into the great hall, where he saw his old bottle standing high up on a shelf; "Ah, ha!" says he to himself; "maybe I won't have you by-and-by."

"Now," says his landlord, "show us your bottle." Mick set it on the floor, and uttered the words. In a moment, the landlord was tumbled on the floor; ladies and gentlemen, servants and all, were running and roaring, and sprawling and kicking and shrieking. Wine-cups and salvers were knocked about in every direction, until the landlord called out: "Stop those two devils, Mick Purcell, or I'll have you hanged!"

"They never shall stop," said Mick, "till I get my own

bottle that I see up there at top of that shelf."

"Give it down to him, give it down to him, before we are all killed!" says the landlord.

Mick put the bottle in his bosom; in jumped the two men into the new bottle, and he carried the bottles home. I need not lengthen my story by telling how he got richer than ever, how his son married his landlord's only daughter, how he and his wife died when they were very old, and how some of the servants, fighting at their wake, broke the bottles; but still the hill has the name upon it—ay, and so 'twill be always Bottle Hill to the end of the world, and so it ought, for it is a strange story.

The Weaver's Son and
the Giant of the White Hill
Jeremiah Curtin

There was once a weaver in Erin who lived at the edge of a wood; and on a time when he had nothing to burn, he went out with his daughter to get fagots for the fire.

They gathered two bundles, and were ready to carry them home, when who should come along but a splendid-looking stranger on horseback. And he said to the weaver: "My good man, will you give me that girl of yours?"

"Indeed then I will not," said the weaver.

"I'll give you her weight in gold," said the stranger, and he put out the gold there on the ground.

So the weaver went home with the gold and without the daughter. He buried the gold in the garden, without letting his wife know what he had done. When she asked, "Where is our daughter?" the weaver said: "I sent her on an errand to a neighbor's house for things that I want."

Night came, but no sight of the girl. The next time he went for fagots, the weaver took his second daughter to the wood; and when they had two bundles gathered, and were ready to go home, a second stranger came on horseback, much finer than the first, and asked the weaver would he give him his daughter.

"I will not," said the weaver.

"Well," said the stranger, "I'll give you her weight in silver if you'll let her go with me;" and he put the silver down before him.

The weaver carried home the silver and buried it in the garden with the gold, and the daughter went away with the man on horseback.

When he went again to the wood, the weaver took his third daughter with him; and when they were ready to go home, a third man came on horseback, gave the weight of the third daughter in copper, and took her away. The weaver buried the copper with the gold and silver.

Now, the wife was lamenting and moaning night and day for her three daughters, and gave the weaver no rest till he told the whole story.

Now, a son was born to them; and when the boy grew up and was going to school, he heard how his three sisters had been carried away for their weight in gold and silver and copper; and every day when he came home he saw how his mother was lamenting and wandering outside in grief through the fields and pits and ditches, so he asked her what trouble was on her; but she wouldn't tell him a word.

At last he came home crying from school one day, and said: "I'll not sleep three nights in one house till I find my three sisters." Then he said to his mother: "Make me three loaves of bread, mother, for I am going on a journey."

Next day he asked had she the bread ready. She said she had, and she was crying bitterly all the time. "I'm going to leave you now, mother," said he; "and I'll come back when I have found my three sisters."

He went away, and walked on till he was tired and hungry; and then he sat down to eat the bread that his mother had given him, when a red-haired man came up and asked him for something to eat. "Sit down here," said the boy. He sat down, and the two ate till there was not a crumb of the bread left.

The boy told of the journey he was on; then the red-haired man said: "There may not be much use in your going, but there are three things that'll serve you,—the sword of sharpness, the cloth of plenty, and the cloak of darkness. No

186

man can kill you while that sword is in your hand; and whenever you are hungry or dry, all you have to do is to spread the cloth and ask for what you'd like to eat or drink, and it will be there before you. When you put on the cloak, there won't be a man or a woman or a living thing in the world that'll see you, and you'll go whatever place you have set your mind on quicker than any wind."

The red-haired man went his way, and the boy travelled on. Before evening a great shower came, and he ran for shelter to a large oak-tree.

When he got near the tree his foot slipped, the ground opened, and down he went through the earth till he came to another country. When he was in the other country he put on the cloak of darkness and went ahead like a blast of wind, and never stopped till he saw a castle in the distance; and soon he was there. But he found nine gates closed before him, and no way to go through. It was written inside the cloak of darkness that his eldest sister lived in the castle.

He was not long at the gate looking in when a girl came to him and said, "Go on out of that; if you don't, you'll be killed."

"Do you go in," said he to the girl, "and tell my sister, the woman of this castle, to come out to me."

The girl ran in; out came the sister, and asked: "Why are you here, and what did you come for?"

"I have come to this country to find my three sisters, who were given away by my father for their weight in gold, silver, and copper; and you are my eldest sister."

She knew from what he said that he was her brother, so she opened the gates and brought him in, saying: "Don't wonder at anything you see in this castle. My husband is enchanted. I see him only at night. He goes off every morning, stays away all day, and comes home in the evening."

The sun went down; and while they were talking, the husband rushed in, and the noise of him was terrible. He came in the form of a ram, ran up stairs, and soon after came down a man.

"Who is this that's with you?" asked he of the wife.

"Oh! that's my brother, who has come from Erin to see me," said she.

Next morning, when the man of the castle was going off in the form of a ram, he turned to the boy and asked, "Will you stay a few days in my castle? You are welcome."

"Nothing would please me better," said the boy; "but I have made a vow never to sleep three nights in one house till I have found my three sisters."

"Well," said the ram, "since you must go, here is something for you." And pulling out a bit of his own wool, he gave it to the boy, saying: "Keep this; and whenever a trouble is on you, take it out, and call on what rams are in the world to help you."

Away went the ram. The boy took farewell of his sister, put on the cloak of darkness, and disappeared. He travelled till hungry and tired, then he sat down, took off the cloak of darkness, spread the cloth of plenty, and asked for meat and drink. After he had eaten and drunk his fill, he took up the cloth, put on the cloak of darkness, and went ahead, passing every wind that was before him, and leaving every wind that was behind.

About an hour before sunset he saw the castle in which his second sister lived. When he reached the gate, a girl came out to him and said: "Go away from that gate, or you'll be killed."

"I'll not leave this till my sister who lives in the castle comes out and speaks to me."

The girl ran in, and out came the sister. When she heard his story and his father's name, she knew that he was her brother, and said: "Come into the castle, but think nothing of what you'll see or hear. I don't see my husband from morning till night. He goes and comes in a strange form, but he is a man at night."

About sunset there was a terrible noise, and in rushed the man of the castle in the form of a tremendous salmon. He went flapping upstairs; but he wasn't long there till he came down a fine-looking man.

"Who is that with you?" asked he of the wife. "I thought you would let no one into the castle while I was gone."

"Oh! this is my brother, who has come to see me," said she.

"If he's your brother, he's welcome," said the man.

They supped, and then slept till morning. When the man of the castle was going out again, in the form of a great salmon, he turned to the boy and said: "You'd better stay here with us a while."

"I cannot," said the boy. "I made a vow never to sleep three nights in one house till I had seen my three sisters. I must go on now and find my third sister."

The salmon then took off a piece of his fin and gave it to the boy, saying: "If any difficulty meets you, or trouble comes on you, call on what salmons are in the sea to come and help you."

They parted. The boy put on his cloak of darkness, and away he went, more swiftly than any wind. He never stopped till he was hungry and thirsty. Then he sat down, spread the cloth of plenty, and ate his fill; when he had eaten, he went on again till near sundown, when he saw the castle where his third sister lived. All three castles were near the sea. Neither sister knew what place she was in, and neither knew where the other two were living.

The third sister took her brother in just as the first and second had done, telling him not to wonder at anything he saw.

They were not long inside when a roaring noise was

heard, and in came the greatest eagle that ever was seen. The eagle hurried upstairs, and soon came down a man.

"Who is that stranger with you?" asked he of the wife. (He, as well as the ram and salmon, knew the boy; he only wanted to try his wife.)

"This is my brother, who has come to see me."

They all took supper and slept that night. When the eagle was going away in the morning, he pulled a feather out of his wing, and said to the boy: "Keep this; it may serve you. If you are ever in straits and want help, call on what eagles are in the world, and they'll come to you."

There was no hurry now, for the third sister was found; and the boy went upstairs with her to examine the country all around, and to look at the sea. Soon he saw a great white hill, and on the top of the hill a castle.

"In that castle on the white hill beyond," said the sister, "lives a giant, who stole from her home the most beautiful young woman in the world. From all parts the greatest heroes and champions and kings' sons are coming to take her away from the giant and marry her. There is not a man of them all who is able to conquer the giant and free the young woman; but the giant conquers them, cuts their heads off, and then eats their flesh. When he has picked the bones clean, he throws them out; and the whole place around the castle is white with the bones of the men that the giant has eaten."

"I must go," said the boy, "to that castle to know can I kill the giant and bring away the young woman."

So he took leave of his sister, put on the cloak of darkness, took his sword with him, and was soon inside the castle. The giant was fighting with champions outside. When the boy saw the young woman he took off his cloak of darkness and spoke to her.

"Oh!" said she, "what can you do against the giant? No man has ever come to the castle without losing his life The giant kills every man; and no one has ever come here so big that the giant did not eat him at one meal."

"And there is no way to kill him?" asked the boy.

"I think not," said she.

"Well, if you'll give me something to eat, I'll stay here; and when the giant comes in, I'll do my best to kill him. But don't let on that I am here."

Then he put on the cloak of darkness, and no one could see him. When the giant came in, he had the bodies of two men on his back. He threw down the bodies and told the young woman to get them ready for his dinner. Then he snuffed around, and said: "There's some one here; I smell the blood of an Erineach."

"I don't think you do," said the young woman; "I can't see any one."

"Neither can I," said the giant; "but I smell a man."

With that the boy drew his sword; and when the giant was struck, he ran in the direction of the blow to give one back; then he was struck on the other side.

They were at one another this way, the giant and the boy with the cloak of darkness on him, till the giant had fifty wounds, and was covered with blood. Every minute he was getting a slash of a sword, but never could give one back. At last he called out: "Whoever you are, wait till to-morrow, and I'll face you then."

So the fighting stopped; and the young woman began to cry and lament as if her heart would break when she saw the state the giant was in. "Oh! you'll be with me no longer; you'll be killed now: what can I do alone without you?" and she tried to please him, and washed his wounds.

"Don't be afraid," said the giant; "this one, whoever he is, will not kill me, for there is no man in the world that can kill me." Then the giant went to bed, and was well in the morning.

Next day the giant and the boy began in the middle of the afternoon. The giant was covered with wounds, and he had not given one blow to the boy, and could not see him, for he was always in his cloak of darkness. So the giant had to ask for rest till the next morning.

While the young woman was washing and dressing the wounds of the giant she cried and lamented all the time, saying: "What'll become of me now? I'm afraid you'll be killed this time; and how can I live here without you?"

"Have no fear for me," said the giant; "I'll put your mind at rest. In the bottom of the sea is a chest locked and bound, in that chest is a duck, in the duck an egg; and I never can be killed unless some one gets the egg from the duck in the chest at the bottom of the sea, and rubs it on the mole that is under my right breast."

While the giant was telling this to the woman to put her mind at rest, who should be listening to the story but the boy in the cloak of darkness. The minute he heard of the chest in the sea, he thought of the salmons. So off he hurried to the seashore, which was not far away. Then he took out the fin that his eldest sister's husband had given him, and called on what salmons were in the sea to bring up the chest with the duck inside, and put it on the beach before him.

He had not long to wait till he saw nothing but salmon, —the whole sea was covered with them, moving to land; and they put the chest out on the beach before him.

But the chest was locked and strong; how could he open it? He thought of the rams; and taking out the lock of wool, said: "I want what rams are in the world to come and break open this chest!"

That minute the rams of the world were running to the seashore, each with a terrible pair of horns on him; and soon they battered the chest to splinters. Out flew the duck, and away she went over the sea.

The boy took out the feather, and said: "I want what eagles are in the world to get me the egg from that duck."

That minute the duck was surrounded by the eagles of the world, and the egg was soon brought to the boy. He put the feather, the wool, and the fin in his pocket, put on the cloak of darkness, and went to the castle on the white hill, and told the young woman, when she was dressing the wounds of the giant again, to raise up his arm.

Next day they fought till the middle of the afternoon. The giant was almost cut to pieces, and called for a cessation.

The young woman hurried to dress the wounds, and he said: "I see you would help me if you could: you are not able. But never fear, I shall not be killed." Then she raised his arm to wash away the blood, and the boy, who was there in his cloak of darkness, struck the mole with the egg. The giant died that minute.

The boy took the young woman to the castle of his third sister. Next day he went back for the treasures of the giant, and there was more gold in the castle than one horse could draw.

They spent nine days in the castle of the eagle with the third sister. Then the boy gave back the feather, and the two went on till they came to the castle of the salmon, where they spent nine more days with the second sister; and he gave back the fin.

When they came to the castle of the ram, they spent fifteen days with the first sister, and had great feasting and enjoyment. Then the boy gave back the lock of wool to the ram, and taking farewell of his sister and her husband, set out for home with the young woman of the white castle, who was now his wife, bringing presents from the three daughters to their father and mother.

At last they reached the opening near the tree, came up through the ground, and went on to where he met the red-haired man. Then he spread the cloth of plenty, asked for every good meat and drink, and called the red-haired man. He came. The three sat down, ate and drank with enjoyment.

When they had finished, the boy gave back to the red-haired man the cloak of darkness, the sword of sharpness, and the cloth of plenty, and thanked him.

"You were kind to me," said the red-haired man; "you gave me of your bread when I asked for it, and told me where you were going. I took pity on you; for I knew you never could get what you wanted unless I helped you. I am the brother of the eagle, the salmon, and the ram."

They parted. The boy went home, built a castle with the treasure of the giant, and lived happily with his parents and wife.

The Haunted Cellar
T. Crofton Croker

There are few people who have not heard of the MacCarthies— one of the real old Irish families, with the true Milesian blood running in their veins, as thick as buttermilk. Many were the clans of this family in the south; as the MacCarthy-more—and the Mac Carthy-reagh – and the MacCarthy of Muskerry; and all of them were noted for their hospitality to strangers, gentle and simple.

But not one of that name, or of any other, exceeded Justin MacCarthy of Ballinacarthy at putting plenty to eat and drink upon his table; and there was a right hearty welcome for everyone who would share it with him. Many a wine-cellar would be ashamed of the name if that at Ballinacarthy was the proper pattern for one; large as that cellar was, it was crowded with bins of wine, and long rows of pipes, and hogsheads, and casks, that it would take more time to count than any sober man could spare in such a place, with plenty to drink about him, and a hearty welcome to do so.

There are many, no doubt, who will think that the butler would have little to complain of in such a house; and the whole country round would have agreed with them, if a man could be found to remain as Mr. MacCarthy's butler for any length of time worth speaking of; yet not one who had been in his service gave him a bad word.

"We have no fault," they would say, "to find with the master; and if he could but get anyone to fetch his wine from the cellar, we might every one of us have grown grey in the house, and have lived quiet and contented enough in his service until the end of our days."

" 'Tis a queer thing that, surely," thought young Jack Leary, a lad who had been brought up from a mere child in the stables of Ballinacarthy to assist in taking care of the horses, and had occasionally lent a hand in the butler's pantry – " 'tis a mighty queer thing, surely, that one man after another cannot content himself with the best place in the house of a good master, but that every one of them must quit, all through the means, as they say, of the wine-cellar. If the master, long life to him! Would but make me his butler, I warrant never the word more would be heard of grumbling at his bidding to go to the wine-cellar."

Young Leary accordingly watched for what he conceived to be a favourable opportunity of presenting himself to the notice of his master.

A few mornings after, Mr. MacCarthy went into his stable-yard rather earlier than usual, and called loudly for the groom to saddle his horse, as he intended going out with the hounds. But there was no groom to answer, and young Jack Leary led Rainbow out of the stable.

"Where is William?" inquired Mr. MacCarthy.

"Sir?" said Jack; and Mr. MacCarthy repeated the question.

"Is it William, please your honour?" returned Jack. "Why, then, to tell the truth, he had just one drop too much last night."

"Where did he get it?" said Mr. MacCarthy; "for since Thomas went away, the key of the wine-cellar has been in my pocket, and I have been obliged to fetch what was drank myself."

"Sorrow a know I know," said Leary, "unless the cook might have given him the least taste in life of whisky. But," continued he, performing a low bow by seizing with his right hand a lock of hair, and pulling down his head by it, whilst his left leg, which had been put forward, was scraped back against the ground, "may I make so bold as just to ask your honour one question?"

"Speak out, Jack," said Mr. MacCarthy.

"Why, then, does your honour want a butler?"

"Can you recommend me one," returned his master, with the smile of good-humour upon his countenance, "and one who will not be afraid of going to my wine-cellar?"

"Is the wine-cellar all the matter?" said young Leary. "Devil a doubt I have of myself then for that."

"So you mean to offer me your services in the capacity of butler?" said Mr. MacCarthy, with some surprise.

"Exactly so!" answered Leary, now for the first time looking up from the ground.

"Well, I believe you to be a good lad, and have no objection to give you a trial."

"Long may your honour reign over us, and the Lord spare you to us!" ejaculated Leary, with another national bow, as his master rode off; and he continued for some time to gaze after him with a vacant stare, which slowly and gradually assumed a look of importance.

"Jack Leary," said he at length, "Jack— is it Jack?" in a tone of wonder. "Faith, 'tis not Jack now, but Mr. John, the butler;" and with an air of becoming consequence, he strode out of the stable-yard towards the kitchen.

It is of little purport to my story, although it may afford an instructive lesson to the reader, to depict the sudden transition of nobody into somebody. Jack's former stable companion, a poor superannuated hound named Bran, who had been accustomed to receive many an affectionate pat on the head, was spurned from him with a kick and an "Out of the way, sirrah." Indeed, poor Jack's memory seemed sadly affected by this sudden change of situation. What established the point beyond all doubt was his almost forgetting the pretty face of Peggy, the kitchen wench, whose heart he had assailed but the preceding week by the offer of purchasing a gold ring for the fourth finger of her right hand, and a lusty imprint of good-will upon her lips.

When Mr. MacCarthy returned from hunting, he sent for Jack Leary—so he still continued to call his new butler. "Jack," said he, "I believe you are a trustworthy lad, and here are the keys of my cellar. I have asked the gentlemen with whom I hunted to-day to dine with me, and I hope they will be satisfied at the way in which you will wait on them at table; but above all, let there be no want of wine after dinner."

Mr. John having a tolerably quick eye for such things, and being naturally a handy lad, spread his cloth accordingly, laid his plates and knives and forks in the same manner he had seen his predecessors in office perform these mysteries, and really, for the first time, got through attendance on dinner very well.

It must not be forgotten, however, that it was at the house of an Irish country squire, who was entertaining a company of booted and spurred fox-hunters, not very particular about what are considered matters of infinite importance under other circumstances and in other societies.

For instance, few of Mr. MacCarthy's guests (though all excellent and worthy men in their way) cared much whether the punch produced after soup was made of Jamaica or Antigua rum; some even would not have been inclined to question the correctness of good old Irish whisky; and, with the exception of their liberal host himself, everyone in company preferred the port which Mr. MacCarthy put on his table to the less ardent flavour of claret— a choice rather at variance with modern sentiment.

It was waxing near midnight when Mr. MacCarthy rang the bell three times. This was a signal for more wine; and Jack proceeded to the cellar to procure a fresh supply, but it must be confessed now without some little hesitation.

The luxury of ice was then unknown in the south of Ireland; but the superiority of cool wine had been acknowledged by all men of sound judgment and true taste.

The grandfather of Mr. MacCarthy, who had built the mansion of Ballinacarthy upon the site of an old castle which had belonged to his ancestors, was fully aware of this important fact; and in the construction of his magnificent wine-cellar, had availed himself of a deep vault, excavated out of the solid rock in former times as a place of retreat and security.

The descent to this vault was by a flight of steep stone stairs, and here and there in the wall were narrow passages—I thought rather to call them crevices; and also certain projections which cast deep shadows, and looked very frightful when anyone went down the cellar stairs with a single light; indeed, two lights did not much improve the matter, for though the breadth of the shadows became less, the narrow crevices remained as dark and darker than ever.

Summoning up all his resolution, down went the new butler, bearing in his right hand a lantern and the key of the cellar, and in his left a basket, which he considered sufficiently capacious to contain an adequate stock for the remainder of the evening. He arrived at the door without any interruption whatever; but when he put the key, which was of an ancient and clumsy kind—for it was before the days of Bramah's patent—and turned it in the lock, he thought he heard a strange kind of laughing within the cellar, to which some empty bottles that stood upon the floor outside vibrated so violently, that they struck against each other: in this he could not be mistaken, although he may have been deceived in the laugh, for the bottles were just at his feet, and he saw them in motion.

Leary paused for a moment, and looked about him with becoming caution. He then boldly seized the handle of the key, and turned it with all his strength in the lock, as if he doubted his own power of doing so; and the door flew open with a most tremendous crash, that, if the house had not been built upon the solid rock, would have shook it from the foundation.

To recount what the poor fellow saw would be impossible, for he seems not to know very clearly himself; but what he told the cook the next morning was, that he heard a roaring and bellowing like a mad bull, and that all the pipes and hogsheads and casks in the cellar went rocking backwards and forwards with so much force, that he thought everyone would have been staved in, and that he should have been drowned or smothered in wine.

When Leary recovered, he made his way back as well as he could to the dining-room, where he found his master and the company very impatient for his return.

"What kept you?" said Mr. MacCarthy, in an angry voice; "and where is the wine? I rung for it half an hour since."

"The wine is in the cellar, I hope, sir," said Jack, trembling violently. "I hope 'tis not all lost."

"What do you mean, fool?" exclaimed Mr. MacCarthy, in a still more angry tone. "Why did you not fetch some with you?"

Jack looked wildly about him, and only uttered a deep groan.

"Gentlemen," said Mr. MacCarthy to his guests, "this is too much. When I next see you to dinner, I hope it will be in another house, for it is impossible I can remain longer in this, where a man has no command over his own wine-cellar, and cannot get a butler to do his duty. I have long thought of moving from Ballinacarthy; and I am now determined, with the blessing of God, to leave it to-morrow. But wine shall you have, were I to go myself to the cellar for it." So saying, he rose from the table, took the key and lantern from his half-stupified servant, who regarded him with a look of vacancy, and descended the narrow stairs, already described, which led to his cellar.

When he arrived at the door, which he found open, he thought he heard a noise, as if of rats or mice scrambling over the casks, and on advancing perceived a little figure, about six inches in height, seated astride upon the pipe of the oldest port in the place, and bearing a spigot upon his shoulder. Raising the lantern, Mr. MacCarthy contemplated the little fellow with wonder: he wore a red nightcap on his head; before him was a short leather apron, which now, from his attitude, fell rather on one side; and he had stockings of a light blue colour, so long as nearly to cover the entire of his legs; with shoes having huge silver buckles in them, and with high heels (perhaps out of vanity to make him appear taller). His face was like a withered winter apple; and his nose, which was of a bright crimson colour, about the tip wore a delicate purple bloom, like that of a plum; yet his eyes twinkled

"like those mites
Of candied dew in moony nights—"

and his mouth twitched up at one side with an arch grin.

"Ha, scoundrel!" exclaimed Mr. MacCarthy, "have I found you at last? Disturber of my cellar—what are you doing there?"

"Sure, and master," returned the little fellow, looking up at him with one eye, and with the other throwing a sly glance towards the spigot on his shoulder, "ain't we going to move to-morrow? and sure, you would not leave your own little Cluricaune Naggeneen behind you?"

"Oh!" thought Mr. MacCarthy, "if you are to follow me, Master Naggeneen, I don't see much use in quitting Ballinacarthy." So filling with wine the basket which young Leary in his fright had left behind him, and locking the cellar door, he rejoined his guests.

For some years after, Mr. MacCarthy had always to fetch the wine for his table himself, as the little Naggeneen seemed to feel a personal respect towards him. Notwithstanding the labour of these journeys, the worthy lord of Ballinacarthy lived in his paternal mansion to a good round age, and was famous to the last for the excellence of his wine and the conviviality of his company; but at the time of his death that same conviviality had nearly emptied his wine-cellar; and as it was never so well filled again, nor so often visited, the revels of Master Naggeneen became less celebrated, and are now only spoken of amongst the legendary lore of the country. It is even said that the poor little fellow took the declension of the cellar so to heart that he became negligent and careless of himself, and that he has been sometimes seen going about with hardly a skreed to cover him.

Some, however, believed that he turned brogue-maker, and assert that they have seen him at his work, and heard him whistling as merry as a blackbird on a May morning, under the shadow of a brown jug of foaming ale, bigger—aye, bigger than himself; decently dressed enough, they say—only looking mighty old. But still 'tis clear he has his wits about him, since no one ever had the luck to catch him, or to get hold of the purse he has with him, which they call *spre-na-skillinagh*, and 'tis said is never without a shilling in it.

The Fisherman's Son and the Gruagach of Tricks

Jeremiah Curtin

There was an old fisherman once in Erin who had a wife and one son.

The old fisherman used to go about with a fishing-rod and tackle to the rivers and lochs and every place where fish resort, and he was killing salmon and other fish to keep the life in himself and his wife and son.

The son was not so keen nor so wise as another, and the father was instructing him every day in fishing, so that if himself should be taken from the world, the son would be able to support the old mother and get his own living.

One day when the father and son were fishing in a

river near the sea, they looked out over the water and saw a small dark speck on the waves. It grew larger and larger, till they saw a boat, and when the boat drew near they saw a man sitting in the stern of it.

There was a nice beach near the place where they were fishing. The man brought the boat straight to the beach, and stepping out drew it up on the sand.

They saw then that the stranger was a man of high degree (*duine uasal*).

After he had put the boat high on the sand, he came to where the two were at work, and said: "Old fisherman, you'd better let this son of yours with me for a year and a day, and I will make a very wise man of him. I am the Gruagach na g-cleasan (Gruagach of tricks), and I'll bind myself to be here with your son this day year."

"I can't let him go," said the old fisherman, "till he gets his mother's advice."

"Whatever goes as far as women I'll have nothing to do with," said the Gruagach. "You had better give him to me now, and let the mother alone."

They talked till at last the fisherman promised to let his son go for the year and a day. Then the Gruagach gave his word to have the boy there at the seashore that day year.

The Gruagach and the boy went into the boat and sailed away.

When the year and a day were over, the old fisherman went to the same place where he had parted with his son and the Gruagach, and stood looking over the sea, thinking would he see his son that day.

At last he saw a black spot on the water, then a boat. When it was near he saw two men sitting in the stern of the boat. When it touched land, the two, who were *duine uasal* in appearance, jumped out, and one of them pulled the boat to the top of the strand. Then that one, followed by the other, came to were the old fisherman was waiting, and asked: "What trouble is on you now, my good man?"

"I had a son that was n't so keen nor so wise as another, and myself and this son were here fishing, and a stranger came, like yourself to-day, and asked would I let my son with him for a year and a day. I let the son go, and the man promised to be here with him to-day, and that's why I am waiting at this place now."

"Well," said the Gruagach, "am I your son?"

"You are not," said the fisherman.

"Is this man here your son?"

"I don't know him," said the fisherman.

Well, then, he is all you will have in place of your son," said the Gruagach.

The old man looked again, and knew his son. He caught hold of him and welcomed him home.

"Now," said the Gruagach, "is n't he a better man than he was a year ago?"

"Oh, he's nearly a smart man now!" said the old fisherman.

"Well," said the Gruagach, "will you let him with me for another year and a day?"

"I will not," said the old man; "I want him myself."

The Gruagach then begged and craved till the fisherman promised to let the son with him for a year and a day again. But the old man forgot to take his word of the Gruagach to bring back the son at the end of the time; and when the Gruagach and the boy were in the boat, and had pushed out to sea, the Gruagach shouted to the old man: "I kept my promise to bring back your son to-day. I have n't given you my word at all now. I'll not bring him back, and you'll never see him again."

The fisherman went home with a heavy and sorrowful heart, and the old woman scolded him all that night till next morning for letting her son go with the Gruagach a second time.

Then himself and the old woman were lamenting a quarter of a year; and when another quarter had passed, he said to her: "I'll leave you here now, and I'll be walking on myself till I wear my legs off up to my knees, and from my knees to my waist, till I find my son."

So away went the old man walking, and he used to

spend but one night in a house, and not two nights in any house, till his feet were all in blisters. One evening late he came to a hut where there was an old woman sitting at a fire.

"Poor man!" said she, when she laid eyes on him, "it's a great distress you are in, to be so disfigured with wounds and sores. What is the trouble that's on you?"

"I had a son," said the old man, "and the Gruagach na g-cleasan came on a day and took him from me."

"Oh, poor man!" said she. "I have a son with that same Gruagach these twelve years, and I have never been able to get him back or get sight of him, and I'm in dread you'll not be able to get your son either. But to-morrow, in the morning, I'll tell you all I know, and show you the road you must go to find the house of the Gruagach na g-cleasan."

Next morning she showed the old fisherman the road. He was to come to the place by evening.

When he came and entered the house, the Gruagach shook hands with him, and said: "You are welcome, old fisher-man. It was I that put this journey on you, and made you come here looking for your son."

"It was no one else but you," said the fisherman.

"Well," said the Gruagach, "you won't see your son to-day. At noon to-morrow I'll put a whistle in my mouth and call together all the birds in my place, and they'll come. Among others will be twelve doves. I'll put my hand in my pocket, this way, and take out wheat and throw it before them on the ground. The doves will eat the wheat, and you must pick your son out of the twelve. If you find him, you'll have him; if you don't, you'll never see him again."

After the Gruagach had said these words the old man ate his supper and went to bed.

In the dead of night the old fisherman's son came. "Oh, father!" said he, "it would be hard for you to pick me out among the twelve doves, if you had to do it alone; but I'll tell you. When the Gruagach calls us in, and we go to pick up the wheat, I'll make a ring around the others, walking for myself; and as I go I'll give some of them a tip of my bill, and I'll lift my wings when I'm striking them. There was a spot under one of my arms when I left home, and you'll see that spot under my wing when I raise it to-morrow. Don't miss the bird that I'll be, and don't let your eyes off it; if you do, you'll lose me forever."

Next morning the old man rose, had his breakfast, and kept thinking of what his son had told him.

At midday the Gruagach took his whistle and blew. Birds came to him from every part, and among others the twelve doves.

He took wheat from his pocket, threw it to the doves, and said to the father: "Now pick out your son from the twelve."

The old man was watching, and soon he saw one of

213

the doves walking around the other eleven and hitting some of them a clip of its bill, and then it raised its wings, and the old man saw the spot. The bird let its wings down again, and went to eating with the rest.

The father never let his eyes off the bird. After a while he said to the Gruagach: "I'll have that bird there for my son."

"Well," said the Gruagach, "that is your son. I can't blame you for having him; but I blame your instructor for the information he gave you, and I give him my curse."

So the old fisherman got his son back in his proper shape, and away they went, father and son, from the house of the Gruagach. The old man felt stronger now, and they never stopped travelling a day till they came home.

The old mother was very glad to see her son, and see him such a wise, smart man.

After coming home they had no means but the fishing; they were as poor as ever before.

At this time it was given out at every cross-road in Erin, and in all public places in the kingdom, that there were to be great horse-races. Now, when the day came, the old fisherman's son said: "Come away with me, father, to the races."

The old man went with him, and when they were near the race-course, the son said: "Stop here till I tell you this: I'll make myself into the best horse that's here to-day, and do you take me to the place where the races are to be, and when you take me in, I'll open my mouth, trying to kill and eat every man that'll be near me, I'll have such life and swiftness; and do you find a rider for me that'll ride me, and don't let me go till the other horses are far ahead on the course. Then let me go. I'll come up to them, and I'll run ahead of them and win the race. After that every rich man there will want to buy me of you; but don't you sell me to any man for less than five hundred pounds; and be sure to get that price for me. And when you have the gold, and you are giving me up, take the bit out of my mouth, and don't sell the bridle for any money. Then come to this spot, shake the bridle, and I'll be here in my own form before you."

The son made himself a horse, and the old fisherman took him to the race. He reared and snorted, trying to take the head off very man that came near him.

The old man shouted for a rider. A rider came; he mounted the horse and held him in. The old man did n't let him start till the other horses were well ahead on the course; then he let him go.

The new horse caught up with the others and shot past them. So they had not gone half way when he was in at the winning-post.

When the race was ended, there was a great noise over the strange horse. Men crowded around the old fisherman from every corner of the field, asking what would he take for the horse.

"Five hundred pounds," said he.

"Here 't is for you," said the next man to him.

In a moment the horse was sold, and the money in the old man's pocket. Then he pulled the bridle off the horse's head, and made his way out of the place as fast as ever he could.

It was not long till he was at the spot where the son had told him what to do. The minute he came, he shook the bridle, and the son was there before him in his own shape and features.

Oh, but the old fisherman was glad when he had his son with him again, and the money in his pocket!

The two went home together. They had money enough now to live, and quit the fishing. They had plenty to eat and drink, and they spent their lives in ease and comfort till the next year, when it was given out at all the cross-roads in Erin, and every public place in the kingdom, that there was to be a great hunting with hound, in the same place where the races had been the year before.

When the day came, the fisherman's son said: "Come, father, let us go away to this hunting."

"Ah!" said the old man, "what do we want to go for? Have n't we plenty to eat at home, with money enough and to spare? What do we care for hunting with hounds?"

"Oh! they'll give us more money," said the son, "if we go."

The fisherman listened to his son, and away they went. When the two came to the spot where the son had made a horse of himself the year before, he stopped, and said to the father: "I'll make a hound of myself to-day, and when you bring me in sight of the game, you'll see me wild with jumping and trying to get away; but do you hold me fast till the right time comes, then let go. I'll sweep ahead of every hound in the field, catch the game, and win the prize for you.

"When the hunt is over, so many men will come to buy me that they'll put you in a maze; but be sure you get three hundred pounds for me, and when you have the money, and are giving me up, don't forget to keep my rope. Come to this place, shake the rope, and I'll be here before you, as I am now. If you don't keep the rope, you'll go home without me."

The son made a hound of himself, and the old father took him to the hunting-ground.

When the hunt began, the hound was springing and jumping like mad; but the father held him till the others were far out in the field. Then he let him loose, and away went the son.

Soon he was up with the pack, then in front of the pack, and never stopped till he caught the game and won the prize.

When the hunt was over, and the dogs and game brought in, all the people crowded around the old fisherman, saying: "What do you want of that hound? Better sell him; he's no good to you."

They put the old man in a maze, there were so many of them, and they pressed him so hard.

He said at last: "I'll sell the hound; and three hundred pounds is the price I want for him."

"Here 't is for you," said a stranger, putting the money into his hand.

The old man took the money and gave up the dog, without taking off the rope. He forgot his son's warning.

That minute the Gruagach na g-cleasan called out: "I'll take the worth of my money out of your son now;" and away he went with the hound.

The old man walked home alone that night, and it is a heavy heart he had in him when he came to the old woman without the son. And the two were lamenting their lot till morning.

Still and all, they were better off than the first time they lost their son, as they had plenty of everything, and could live at their ease.

The Gruagach went away home, and put the fisherman's son in a cave of concealment that he had, bound him hand and foot, and tied hard knots on his neck up to his chin. From above there fell on him drops of poison, and every drop that fell went from the skin to the flesh to the bone, from the bone to the marrow, and he sat there under the poison drops, without meat, drink, or rest.

In the Gruagach's house was a servant-maid, and the fisherman's son had been kind to her the time he was in the place before.

On a day when the Gruagach and his eleven sons were out hunting, the maid was going with a tub of dirty water to throw it into the river that ran by the side of the house. She went through the cave of concealment where the fisherman's son was bound, and he asked of her the wetting of his mouth from the tub.

"Oh! the Gruagach would take the life of me," said she, "when he comes home, if I gave you as much as one drop."

"Well," said he, "when I was in this house before, and when I had power in my hands, it's good and kind I was to you; and when I get out of this confinement I'll do you a turn, if you give me the wetting of my mouth now,"

The maid put the tub near his lips.

"Oh! I can't stoop to drink unless you untie one knot from my throat," said he.' Then she put the tub down, stooped to him, and loosed one knot from his throat. When she loosed the one knot he made an eel of himself, and dropped into the tub. There he began shaking the water, till he put some of it on the ground, and when he had the place about him wet, he sprang from the tub, and slipped along out under the door. The maid caught him; but could not hold him, he was so slippery. He made his way from the door to the river, which ran near the side of the house.

When the Gruagach na g-cleasan came home in the evening with his eleven sons, they went to take a look at the fisherman's son; but he was not to be seen.

Then the Gruagach called the maid, and taking his sword, said: "I'll take the head off you if you don't tell me this minute what happened while I was gone."

"Oh!" said the maid, "he begged so hard for a drop of dirty water to wet his mouth that I had n't the heart to refuse, for 't is good he was to me and kind each time he saw me when he was here in the house before. When the water touched his mouth, he made an eel of himself, spilled water out of the tub, and slipped along over the wet place to the river outside. I caught him to bring him back, but I could n't hold him; in spite of all I could do, he made away."

The Gruagach dropped his sword, and went to the water side with his sons.

The sons made eleven eels of themselves, and the Gruagach their father was the twelfth. They went around in the water, searching in every place, and there was not a stone in the river that they passed without looking under and around it for the old fisherman's son.

And when he knew that they were after him, he made himself into a salmon, the sons made eleven otters of themselves, and the Gruagach made himself the twelfth.

When the fisherman's son found that twelve otters were after him, he was weak with hunger, and when they had come near, he made himself a whale. But the eleven brothers and their father made twelve cannon whales of themselves, for they had all gone out of the river, and were in the sea now.

When they were coming near him, the fisherman's son was weak from pursuit and hunger, so he jumped up out of the water, and made a swallow of himself; but the Gruagach and his sons became twelve hawks, and chased the swallow through the air; and as they whirled round and darted, they pressed him hard, till all of them came near the castle of the king of Erin.

Now the king had a summer-house for his daughter; and where should she be at this time but sitting on the top of the summer-house.

The old fisherman's son dropped down till he was near her; then he fell into her lap in the form of a ring. The daughter of the king of Erin took up the ring, looked at it, and put it on her finger. The ring took her fancy, and she was glad.

When the Gruagach and his sons saw this, they let themselves down at the king's castle, having the form of the finest men that could be seen in the kingdom.

When the king's daughter had the ring on her finger she looked at it and liked it. Then the ring spoke, and said: "My life is in your hands now; don't part from the ring, and don't let it go to any man, and you'll give me a long life."

The Gruagach na g-cleansan and his eleven sons went into the king's castle and played on every sport that should be shown before a king. This they did for three days and three nights. When that time was over, and they were going away, the king spoke up and asked:

"What is the reward that you would like, and what would be pleasing to you from me?"

"We want neither gold nor silver," said the Gruagach; "all the reward we ask of you is the ring that I lost on a time, and which is now on your daughter's finger."

"If my daughter has the ring that you lost, it shall be given to you," said the king.

Now the ring spoke to the king's daughter and said: "Don't part with me for anything till you send your trusted man for three gallons of strong spirits and a gallon of wheat; put the spirits and the wheat together in an open barrel before the fire. When your father says you must give up the ring, do you answer back that you have never left the summer-house, that you have nothing on your hand but what is your own and paid for. Your father will say then that you must part with me, and give me up to the stranger. When he forces you in this way, and you can keep me no longer, then throw me into the fire; and you'll see great sport and strange things."

The king's daughter sent for the spirits and the wheat,

had them mixed together, and put in an open barrel before the fire.

The king called the daughter in, and asked: "Have you the ring which this stranger lost?"

"I have a ring," said she, "but it's my own, and I'll not part with it. I'll not give it to him nor to any man."

"You must," said the king, "for my word is pledged, and you must part with the ring!"

When she heard this, she slipped the ring from her finger and threw it into the fire.

That moment the eleven brothers made eleven pairs of tongs of themselves; their father, the old Gruagach, was the twelfth pair.

The twelve jumped into the fire to know in what spark of it would they find the old fisherman's son; and they were a long time working and searching through the fire, when out flew a spark, and into the barrel.

The twelve made themselves men, turned over the barrel, and spilled the wheat on the floor. Then in a twinkling they were twelve cocks strutting around.

They fell to and picked away at the wheat to know which one would find the fisherman's son. Soon one dropped on one side, and second on the opposite side, until all twelve were lying drunk from the wheat.

Then the old fisherman's son made a fox of himself,

and the first cock he came to was the old Gruagach na g-cleas-an himself. He took the head off the Gruagach with one bite, and the heads off the eleven brothers with eleven other bites.

When the twelve were dead, the old fisherman's son made himself the finest-looking man in Erin, and began to give music and sport to the king; and he entertained him five times better than had the Gruagach and his eleven sons.

Then the king's daughter fell in love with him, and she set her mind on him to that degree that there was no life for her without him.

When the king saw the straits that his daughter was in, he ordered the marriage without delay.

The wedding lasted for nine days and nine nights, and the ninth night was the best of all.

When the wedding was over, the king felt he was losing his strength, so he took the crown off his own head, and put it on the head of the old fisherman's son, and made him king of Erin in place of himself.

The young couple were the luck, and we the stepping-stones. The presents we got at the marriage were stockings of buttermilk and shoes of paper, and these were worn to the soles of our feet when we got home from the wedding.

The Little Shoe
T. Crofton Croker

"**N**ow, tell me, Molly," said Mr. Coote to Molly Cogan, as he met her on the road one day, close to one of the old gateways of Kilmallock, "did you ever hear of the Cluricaune?"

"Is it the Cluricaune? Why, then, sure I did, often and often; many's the time I heard my father—rest his soul!—tell about 'em."

"But did you ever see one, Molly, yourself?"

"Och! no, I never see one in my life; but my grandfather, that's my father's father, you know, he see one, one time, and caught him too."

"Caught him! Oh, Molly, tell me how?"

"Why, then, I'll tell you. My grandfather, you see, was

out there above in the bog, drawing home turf, and the poor old mare was tired after her day's work, and the old man went out to the stable to look after her, and to see if she was eating her hay; and when he came to the stable door there, my dear, he heard something hammering, hammering, hammering, just for all the world like a shoemaker making a shoe, and whistling all the time the prettiest tune he ever heard in his whole life before. Well, my grandfather, he thought it was the Cluricaune, and he said to himself, says he, 'I'll catch you, if I can, and then I'll have money enough always.' So he opened the door very quietly, and didn't make a bit of noise in the world that ever was heard, and looked all about, but never a bit of the little man he could see anywhere, but he heard him hammering and whistling, and so he looked and looked, till at last he see the little fellow; and where was he, do you think, but in the girth under the mare, and there he was with his little bit of an apron on him, and hammer in his hand, and a little red nightcap on his head, and he making a shoe, and he was so busy with his work, and he was hammering and whistling so loud, that he never minded my grandfather till he caught him fast in his hand. 'Faith, I have you now,' says he, 'and I'll never let you go till I get your purse, that's what I won't, so give it here to me at once now.' 'Stop, stop,' says the Cluricaune; 'stop, stop,' says he, 'till I get it for you.' So my grandfather, like a fool, you see, opened his hand a little, and the little fellow jumped away laughing, and he never saw him any more, and the never the bit of the purse did he get, only the Cluricaune left his little shoe that he was making, and my grandfather was mad enough angry with himself for letting him go; but he had the shoe all his life, and my own mother told me she often see it, and had it in her hand, and 'twas the prettiest little shoe she ever saw."

"And did you see it yourself, Molly?"

"Oh, no, my dear! It was lost long afore I was born; but my mother told me about it often and often enough."

Jamie Freel
and the Young Lady
Letitia Maclintock

Down in Fannet, in times gone
by, lived Jamie Freel and his mother. Jamie was the widow's
sole support; his strong arm worked for her untiringly, and as
each Saturday night came round, he poured his wages into her
lap, thanking her dutifully for the halfpence which she
returned to him for tobacco.

He was extolled by his neighbours, of whose opinion
he was ignorant—neighbours who lived pretty close to him,
whom he had never seen, who are, indeed, rarely seen by
mortals, except on May eves and Halloweens.

An old ruined castle, about a quarter of a mile from his

cabin, was said to be the abode of the "wee folk". Every Halloween were the ancient windows lighted up, and passers-by saw little figures flitting to and fro inside the building, while they heard the music of pipes and flutes.

It was well known that fairy revels took place; but nobody had the courage to intrude on them.

Jamie had often watched the little figures from a distance, and listened to the charming music, wondering what the inside of the castle was like; but one Halloween he got up and took his cap, saying to his mother, "I'm awa' to the castle to seek my fortune."

"What!" cried she, "would you venture there? you that's the poor widow's one son! Dinna be sae venturesome an' foolitch, Jamie! They'll kill you, an' then what'll come o' me?"

"Never fear, mother; nae harm 'ill happen me, but I maun gae."

He set out, and as he crossed the potato-field, came in sight of the castle, whose windows were ablaze with light, that seemed to turn the russet leaves, still clinging to the crab-tree branches, into gold.

Halting in the grove at one side of the ruin, he listened to the elfin revelry, and the laughter and singing made him all the more determined to proceed.

Numbers of little people, the largest about the size of a child of five years old, were dancing to the music of flutes and fiddles, while others drank and feasted.

"Welcome, Jamie Freel! welcome, welcome, Jamie!" cried the company, perceiving their visitor. The word "Welcome" was caught up and repeated by every voice in the castle.

Time flew, and Jamie was enjoying himself very much, when his hosts said, "We're going to ride to Dublin tonight to steal a young lady. Will you come too, Jamie Freel?"

"Aye, that will I!" cried the rash youth, thirsting for adventure.

A troop of horses stood at the door. Jamie mounted and his steed rose with him into the air. He was presently flying over his mother's cottage, surrounded by the elfin troop, and on and on they went, over bold mountains, over little hills, over the deep Lough Swilley, over towns and cottages, when people were burning nuts, and eating apples, and keeping merry Halloween. It seemed to Jamie that they flew all round Ireland before they got to Dublin.

"This is Derry," said the fairies, flying over the cathedral spire; and what was said by one voice was repeated by all the rest, till fifty little voices were crying out, "Derry! Derry! Derry!"

In like manner was Jamie informed as they passed over each town on the route, and at length he heard the silvery voices cry, "Dublin! Dublin!"

It was no mean dwelling that was to be honoured by the fairy visit, but one of the finest houses in Stephen's Green.

The troop dismounted near a window, and Jamie saw a beautiful face, on a pillow in a splendid bed. He saw the young lady lifted and carried away, while the stick which was dropped in her place on the bed took her exact form.

The lady was placed before one rider and carried a short way, then given another, and the names of the towns were cried out as before.

They were approaching home. Jamie heard "Rathmullan", "Milford", "Tamney", and then he knew they were near his own house.

"You've all had your turn at carrying the young lady," said he. "Why wouldn't I get her for a wee piece?"

"Ay, Jamie," replied they, pleasantly, "you may take your turn at carrying her, to be sure."

Holding his prize very tightly, he dropped down near his mother's door.

"Jamie Freel, Jamie Freel! is that the way you treat us?" cried they, and they too dropped down near the door.

Jamie held fast, though he knew not what he was holding, for the little folk turned the lady into all sorts of strange shapes. At one moment she was a big black dog, barking and trying to bite; at another, a glowing bar of iron, which yet had no heat; then, again, a sack of wool.

But still Jamie held her, and the baffled elves were turning away, when a tiny woman, the smallest of the party, exclaimed, "Jamie Freel has her awa' frae us, but he sall hae nae gude o' her, for I'll mak' her deaf and dumb," and she threw something over the young girl.

While they rode off disappointed, Jamie lifted the latch and went in.

"Jamie, man!" cried his mother, "you've been awa' all night; what have they done on you?"

"Naething bad, mother; I ha' the very best of gude luck. Here's a beautiful young lady I ha' brought you for company."

"Bless us an' save us!" exclaimed the mother, and for some minutes she was so astonished that she could not think of anything else to say.

Jamie told his story of the night's adventure, ending by saying, "Surely you wouldna have allowed me to let her gang with them to be lost forever?"

"But a lady, Jamie! How can a lady eat we'er poor diet, and live in we'er poor way? I ax you that, you foolitch fellow?"

"Weel, mother, sure it's better for her to be here nor over yonder," and he pointed in the direction of the castle.

Meanwhile, the deaf and dumb girl shivered in her light clothing, stepping close to the humble turf fire.

"Poor crathur, she's quare and handsome! Nae wonder they set their hearts on her," said the old woman, gazing at her guest with pity and admiration. "We maun dress her first; but what, in the name o' fortune, hae I fit for the likes o' her to wear?"

She went to her press in "the room", and took out her Sunday gown of brown drugget; she then opened a drawer and drew forth a pair of white stockings, a long snowy garment of fine linen, and a cap, her "dead dress", as she called it.

These articles of attire had long been ready for a certain triste ceremony, in which she would some day fill the chief part, and only saw the light occasionally, when they were hung out to air; but she was willing to give even these to the fair trembling visitor, who was turning in dumb sorrow and wonder from her to Jamie, and from Jamie back to her.

The poor girl suffered herself to be dressed, and then sat down on a "creepie" in the chimney corner, and buried her face in her hands.

"What'll we do to keep up a lady like thou?" cried the old woman.

"I'll work for you both, mother," replied the son.

"An' how could a lady live on we'er poor diet?" she repeated.

"I'll work for her," was all Jamie's answer.

He kept his word. The young lady was very sad for a long time, and tears stole down her cheeks many an evening while the old woman spun by the fire, and Jamie made salmon

233

nets, an accomplishment lately acquired by him, in hopes of adding to the comfort of the guest.

But she was always gentle, and tried to smile when she perceived them looking at her; and by degrees she adapted herself to their ways and mode of life. It was not very long before she began to feed the pig, mash potatoes and meal for the fowls, and knit blue worsted socks.

So a year passed, and Halloween came round again. "Mother," said Jamie, taking down his cap, "I'm off to the ould castle to seek my fortune."

"Are you mad, Jamie?" cried his mother, in terror; "sure they'll kill you this time for what you done on them last year."

Jamie made light of her fears and went his way.

As he reached the crab-tree grove, he saw bright lights in the castle windows as before, and heard loud talking. Creeping under the window, he heard the wee folk say, "That was a poor trick Jamie Freel played us this night last year, when he stole the nice young lady from us."

"Ay," said the tiny woman, "an' I punished him for it, for there she sits, a dumb image by his hearth; but he does na' know that three drops out o' this glass I hold in my hand was give her her hearing and her speeches back again."

Jamie's heart beat fast as he entered the hall. Again he was greeted by a chorus of welcomes from the company— "Here comes Jamie Freel! welcome, welcome, Jamie!"

As soon as the tumult subsided, the little woman said, "You be to drink our health, Jamie, out o' this glass in my hand."

Jamie snatched the glass from her and darted to the door. He never knew how he reached his cabin, but he arrived there breathless, and sank on a stove by the fire.

"You're kilt surely this time, my poor boy," said his mother.

"No, indeed, better luck than ever this time!" and he gave the lady three drops of the liquid that still remained at the bottom of the glass, notwithstanding his mad race over the potato-field.

The lady began to speak, and her first words were words of thanks to Jamie.

The three inmates of the cabin had so much to say to one another, that long after cock-crow, when the fairy music had quite ceased, they were talking round the fire.

"Jamie," said the lady, "be pleased to get me paper and pen and ink, that I may write to my father, and tell him what has become of me."

She wrote, but weeks passed, and she received no answer. Again and again she wrote, and still no answer.

At length she said, "You must come with me to Dublin, Jamie, to find my father."

"I ha' no money to hire a car for you," he replied, "an'

how can you travel to Dublin on your foot?"

But she implored him so much that he consented to set out with her, and walk all the way from Fannet to Dublin. It was not as easy as the fairy journey; but at last they rang the bell at the door of the house in Stephen's Green.

"Tell my father that his daughter is here," said she to the servant who opened the door.

"The gentleman that lives here has no daughter, my girl. He had one, but she died better than a year ago."

"Do you not know me, Sullivan?"

"No, poor girl, I do not."

"Let me see the gentleman. I only ask to see him."

"Well, that's not much to ax; we'll see what can be done."

In a few moments the lady's father came to the door.

"Dear father," said she, "don't you know me?"

"How dare you call me father?" cried the old gentle-man, angrily. "You are an impostor. I have no daughter."

"Look in my face, father, and surely you'll remember me."

"My daughter is dead and buried. She died a long, long time ago," The old gentleman's voice changed from anger to sorrow. "You can go," he concluded.

"Stop, dear father, till you look at this ring on my finger. Look at your name and mine engraved on it."

"It certainly is my daughter's ring; but I do not know how you came by it I fear in no honest way."

"Call my mother, she will be sure to know me," said the poor girl, who, by this time, was crying bitterly.

"My poor wife is beginning to forget her sorrow. She seldom speaks of her daughter now. Why should I renew her grief by reminding her of her loss?"

But the young lady persevered till at last the mother was sent for.

"Mother," she began, when the old lady came to the door, " don't you know your daughter?"

"I have no daughter; my daughter died and was buried a long, long time ago."

"Only look in my face, and surely you'll know me."

The old lady shook her head.

"You have all forgotten me; but look at this mole on my neck. Surely, mother, you know me now?"

"Yes, yes," said the mother, "my Gracie had a mole on her neck like that; but then I saw her in her coffin, and saw the lid shut down upon her."

It became Jamie's turn to speak, and he gave the history of the fairy journey, of the theft of the young lady, of the figure he had seen laid in its place, of her life with his mother in Fannet, of last Halloween, and of the three drops that had released her from her enchantment.

237

She took up the story when he paused, and told how kind the mother and son had been to her.

The parents could not make enough of Jamie. They treated him with every distinction, and when he expressed his wish to return to Fannet, said they did not know what to do to show their gratitude.

But an awkward complication arose. The daughter would not let him go without her. "If Jamie goes, I'll go too," she said. "He saved me from the fairies, and has worked for me ever since. If it had not been for him, dear father and mother, you would never have seen me again. If he goes, I'll go too."

This being her resolution, the old gentleman said that Jamie should become his son-in-law. The mother was brought from Fannet in a coach and four, and there was a splendid wedding.

They all lived together in the grand Dublin house, and Jamie was heir to untold wealth at his father-in-law's death.

The Black Lamb

Lady Wilde

It is a custom among the people, when throwing away water at night to cry out in a loud voice, "Take care of the water," or literally, from the Irish, "Away with yourself from the water"—for they say the spirits of the dead last buried are then wandering about, and it would be dangerous if the water fell on them.

One dark night a woman suddenly threw out a pail of boiling water without thinking of the warning words. Instantly a cry was heard, as of a person in pain, but no one was seen. However, the next night a black lamb entered the house, having the back all fresh scalded, and it lay down moaning by the hearth and died. Then they all knew that this was the spirit that had been scalded by the woman, and they carried the dead lamb out reverently, and buried it deep in the earth. Yet every night at the same hour it walked again into the house, and lay down, moaned, and died: and after this had happened many times, the priest was sent for, and finally, by the strength of his exorcism, the spirit of the dead was laid to rest; the black lamb appeared no more. Neither was the body of the dead lamb found in the grave when they searched for it, though it had been laid by their own hands deep in the earth and covered with clay.